Hiroshima

Memories of a Survivor

*A personal account of the aftermath of the 1945
nuclear bombing of Hiroshima.*

Sachi Komura Rummel

The front cover shows Sachi and Charles in 1965, the year they
were married, as they stand in front of the Peace Dome
remembering the bomb victims.
This building was the target for the atomic bomb dropped on
Hiroshima and is a designated world heritage site.

love and peace

愛 と 平和

Sachi Rummel

幸

TABLE OF CONTENTS

~ iv ~

Acknowledgments

My heartfelt appreciation to the following people:

My husband, Charles and daughter, Lisa, for their ongoing support.

Yumiko Takase and my daughter, Tami, for their assistance in translating Japanese to English.

My sisters-in-law, Sally and Emily for their help with the many edits of the manuscript.

Dr. Eiichiro Ochiai for his special submission on atomic bombs and nuclear radiation.

Overall book advice from Keigo Hirano and Kiyoshi Shimada.

Mr. Ochiba, curator of the Hiroshima Peace Memorial Museum who gave his kind permission to include photographs from the museum.

Geraldine Guilfoile and Rod Baker for helping with the editing and preparation of the manuscript.

Sharon Brownlie
Formatting - aspirebookcovers.com

Lynne Fellows
Editor - Spainify@gmail.com

And last but not least, Fumiko Yamamoto for the cover design.

Foreword

I was eight years old when the atomic bomb was dropped on Hiroshima. By some miracle I survived and decided to write about my experiences in the hope that young people may come to understand the effects of nuclear weapons. Each of us must do our small part to prevent repeating these awful mistakes.

After keeping silent for many years, the 2011 nuclear tragedy in Fukushima spurred me to talk about my experiences. I was greatly supported in writing this book by my husband Charles who has given me unfailing support all the years of our relationship and who was never put off by the obstacles that others saw to a union such as ours.

I am grateful to my sister in law, Sally Kunz who encouraged me to write down my story after the Fukushima earthquake brought the attention of the world once again to the havoc that nuclear radiation can cause.

"I was thinking intensely about you this morning," wrote Sally. *"The sun was shining on the ocean, the sandy beach bright, and the tide*

low. We had been alerted that debris from the enormous tidal wave created by the Fukushima earthquake was about to hit our shores on Vancouver Island.

With encouragement from Sally and others, I began to write this book, which tells my story of growing up in Japan before and after the bomb that changed our lives forever. It is a story of family survival, explains how I came to Canada, met my husband, and how we overcame the challenges of joining east and west.

2018 marks the 73rd anniversary of the dropping of the atomic bomb. Many of the survivors are no longer with us. I dedicate this book to all those who lost their lives from that terrible event.

Sachi Komura Rummel

Prologue

These pages are a sketch of the life of one person – Sachi Komura Rummel. They concern the family she grew up with, her experience as a victim of the Hiroshima atomic bomb, loss of her father, her meeting with Charles – her husband, and her new life in Canada.

Having lived seven years in Fukushima prior to the Tohoku earthquake and meltdown of the nuclear reactor, I have encountered numerous young residents of the area exposed to radiation, experiencing health problems both real and imagined as well as social stigma similar to the victims of Hiroshima. Young people approaching marriageable age experience being *unacceptable* from the families of their potential partners, as Sachi did.

We pray for a future where human beings shall no longer have to suffer the effects of atomic radiation.

Charles Rummel

PART ONE

Letter to My Father
Who Lives in Heaven

My Dear Father,

The town of Hiroshima was destroyed when the Americans dropped the atomic bomb on the 6th of August 1945, at 8:15 in the morning. Late that night, you came home through the burning fire, the collapsed town, across the rivers, stepping over dead bodies. After that, you suffered in bed for ten days until you died.

I was eight years old. I really wanted to play with you, so I came to see you in your bedroom.

"Let's play, Dad!" I said. Your suffering

face was transformed into a smile and you nodded but couldn't say anything.

Dear Father, I remember when you and I were together especially at dinnertime. I sat on your lap and you fed me your snacks, your soup and your scraps. I climbed up on your back or came to the front of you, and you always picked me up on your lap. It was the best time of my day to be with you. I still recall your breath that smelled of beer and sake and your hairy hands and legs. I loved those precious moments but when I think of you, the trauma of the atomic bomb shock still rises into my mind.

Seventy-three years have passed since the atomic bomb was dropped on Hiroshima. ***"Let all the souls here rest in peace, for we shall not repeat the evil,"*** reads the memorial monument at the Hiroshima City of Peace Dome. "We," refers to all of humanity and "the error" of war. This simple inscription on the monument reflects and captures Hiroshima's heartfelt desire to attain world peace. After a long period of silence, I decided to speak up at a public gathering about my experience of living through the aftermath of the first atomic bomb explosion in history. Until now, it has been a very painful and emotional time for me to speak up about this tragedy. However many survivors of Hiroshima and Nagasaki, including myself, are getting close to the end of our lives.

I would like to tell you the story of my life, its turning points and, in particular, of the deeply-rooted effect being a survivor of an atomic bomb has had on my world.

Two Mothers

My father, Kazuo grew up in a family of sake brewers in Hiroshima. However, he was unable to carry on the family factory business of brewing sake. During the war the demand for alcohol literally dried up. People could no longer afford the luxury of enjoying a cup of sake. Instead, he found employment with a local electric company. While he was working there as an office manager, he married Yoshiko and they adopted me as their young child. They were a very happy loving couple. Kazuo's mother, Chizu, was also living with us in an adjoining house.

In those days most married women wore the kimono but Yoshiko, being a modern lady, preferred to wear western dresses. I remember them sitting in armchairs after dinner every night listening to records. But their sweet married life wasn't to continue very long because Yoshiko came down with tuberculosis which was a terrible illness at that time. One of the effects was that she was unable to have children.

When I was five years old, she passed away. Unfortunately I don't have much memory of being with her because tuberculosis was contagious and most of the time she was isolated. In 1943, Kazuo remarried. His second wife became my new mother. Her name was Misao. Their marriage ceremony was held at her house, which was also a sake factory in Hagi City not so far from Hiroshima.

I vividly remember the day they married for I was so excited to have a new mother. I was taken to meet Misao who at that moment was putting on makeup in front of a mirror. I peeked around the corner behind her and first saw her in the reflection of the mirror.

'How beautiful she is, my new mother,' I thought. I was too shy to say hello to her but, unexpectedly, she looked at me and said, "Hi, Sachi. You are Sachi, aren't you? I am your mother. I'll be kind and tender and take care of you."

Just hearing her voice made me happy. Like

an excited pet, I began skipping and jumping around her. I went with them on their honeymoon. It was a favourite story among my relatives. They would laugh saying, "Kazuo took Sachi on the honeymoon."

My dad, Kazuo, took me along because he loved me so much and wanted us to be together.

Misao was a faithful and obedient wife. She was protected by her husband, Kazuo, and was always busy as a homemaker of the Shindo family. I remember that she wore a white apron every day to do house chores from early morning until late at night. When my father left home for work she always polished his shoes and went to the entrance door to open it for him saying, "Goodbye, take care my dear," and bowed to him. When he arrived back from his work usually he shouted, "Here, I am home." She opened the door, bowed, and said, "Welcome home," to my father. It was a beautiful ritual for me, seeing them every morning and every night.

Misao was a good cook. During the wartime, there was hardly any food in the market and the community was controlled by the distribution system of the Japanese government. Because of the war everyone was short of food except farmers. But my father often got some food on the black market and brought it home for us. My mother hesitated to cook this food because the delicious smell might spread around the neighbourhood and others may understand my father had black market food.

During the wartime, the house had no interior decoration. But my mother always decorated it with some flowers. She used flowers from the field and blooms from bushes to arrange natural beauty in the corner of the house. Those flower arrangements gave us peace of mind and serenity during the horrible time of war.

In March 1945, my brother, Yuta was born. That day, the midwife and several neighbours ordered me to leave. "Get out of here! We are so busy. Now be quiet!"

I was taken away to my playroom, but being so curious about what was going on the other side of the door, I stayed quiet and listened with my ear pressed against the door.

Suddenly I heard a baby crying. People were saying, "It's a boy, a boy, a baby boy is born!"

'Oh, my new brother, I have a new brother,' I thought to myself. I was so excited at that moment.

Yuta was born in the middle of the Second World War and all families were poor and suffered from a shortage of food. We were all very thrifty and had to donate gold, silver, and copper to the government for making weapons for the war. My father, Kazuo was a very resourceful man who somehow always found some treats to bring home. We were fortunate to have food to eat every day. Thus, Mom was able to nurse Yuta well.

Meanwhile, my aunt Chieko who was the youngest sister of Kazuo, was evacuated from her hometown and started to live with us. Her husband, Yoshiaki was called to serve in the army. Their son, my three-year-old cousin, Yoshi, became a new playmate. There were seven of us in the family: my grandma, my father, my mother, Aunt Chieko, cousin, Yoshi, my two-month-old younger brother, Yuta and me. Our place had an underground shelter, so we all felt safe.

My Father Kazuo Shindo

My father Kazuo Shindo was working at the Naganuma Electric Company located in downtown Hiroshima. He loved his family so much and was a hard worker. When he came home from his work, he helped my mother in the kitchen as well as in the garden, cutting wood, trimming hedges, and planting vegetables. The neighbours were envious of my mother and said, "How lucky you are, to have such a great husband!"

My father loved his daughter dearly, so I was constantly spoiled. I was the apple of his eye.

My name, Sachi, means "Happiness" in Japanese. He gave me this name wishing me to be a happy girl all of my life. I would say, "YES! I am super happy. All my life."

He was tall and wore a pair of glasses, probably an average businessman but I believed he was so handsome and could do anything he wanted. My father was my idol.

I was not good at mathematics. When I started learning multiplication, I couldn't figure it out. It took a long time to finish my homework. So my father started doing it for me instead of teaching me. I am still bad at mathematics.

Our house was located in the suburb of the City of Hiroshima called Takasu town. There was a creek in front of the house. After the rainy season, fish came down from the mountain stream that we could catch with our hands or with a net. This was a fun game catching carp and eels after school in order to supplement our meals. After the rainy season finished, the hot summer started with the sound of cicadas. Little did I know that these days of innocence were about to come to an end.

Sachi with her friends, Hiroko and Fumiko

The Day the Earth Stood Still

The 6th of August 1945 was a hot, fine summer day. A beautifully clear, cloudless blue sky spread before us as far as the eye could see. My family of seven was living together happily.

Unknown to us at this time, early in the morning, the American B29 bomber, Enola Gay was carrying "Little Boy," the world's first atomic bomb, towards Hiroshima City. Enola Gay was named after the mother of the captain on board the B29 – Colonel Tibbets.

The citizens of Hiroshima were beginning their daily tasks; some were eating breakfast, children were on their way to school, and I was in the schoolyard playing with my classmates. The school playground was about three-and-a-half kilometres from ground zero. As an eight-year-old child, I didn't understand the stark fear of war. I recall people around me talking about the misery that dropping bombs had caused. But even now, I remember the instant the atomic bomb dropped.

The playground was located on top of a small rise. In the school grounds there was a large tree. I am sure that the reason I was not injured was because I was in the shade of that tree. Suddenly, there was a flash of light instantly followed by a blast that created a sandstorm. At first, I couldn't see anything. We were terrified. What had happened? We started running toward the classrooms that were on the ground level.

Our teacher told us to sit down in our own chairs and to be quiet. It took a while to calm down and stop crying. The teacher divided us into small groups to go home following the senior grade group leader. We went home down the mountain by holding hands in pairs.

Black Rain

Along the way back home from school, even though the sky was perfectly clear, a black rain began to fall. My friend Fujita and I somehow became separated from the group. We ducked into an air raid shelter to get cover from the rain. Black rain continued for 40 minutes with thunder and sometimes, large drops of black rain or drizzle. We decided to carry on and descended the mountain anxiously. I don't know how we made it home.

On my way, I stepped into a bucket of fertilizer at the corner of a farmer's house. My foot was a smelly mess. Sobbing nonstop, I washed it in a stream before continuing to make my way home. I met a farmer. He said to me, "Don't cry! You are Japanese. Be strong!"

The other children had already returned home by this time, but our whereabouts were still unknown, and it seemed that the whole community was searching for us. The black rain had dirtied the white blouse I wore that day. The stain never came out even after washing it several times. I really liked that white blouse.

Fortunately, my house in Takasu wasn't burned but the blast had caused the straw tatami mats to buckle. The house was tilted, glass doors were shattered, and some roof tiles had blown off. As there was a well and water pump in the yard, there was no concern about lack of water. Even though the house was damaged, it still kept out the rain and wind. Out in the garden that evening, my grandma filled the washbasin up to my waist with lukewarm water from the pump. I could see the eastern sky painted a mad red.

"That's the town of Hiroshima burning, hey? It's terrible. It looks like a big bomb has fallen. Scary!"

This was the explanation I received.

Ghosts

As the day was coming to an end, the victims of the burned city were being evacuated to the less damaged west side of the city which was supposed to be safe and had lots of clean water with space for those wounded victims. Their burnt clothes were raggedly hanging from their bodies. Their peeled skin was hanging from their hands. Their hair was sticking up in the air or messy. No one could recognize who was who. They were swaying left and right, weeping, crying, and mourning. The ghost-like figures trudged along with burnt rags as clothing, their bodies swollen with burns. As I watched, one person who was walking slowly fell down dead.

Our neighbours were coming to our house to get water from the pump, which was the only supply in our neighbourhood. They were talking with hushed voices. I was kept inside the house while my Grandma prayed *Namuamidabutsu*, a Buddhist prayer. The next-door neighbour, Mr.

Satou came home. So now we had a little hope that my father and my aunt Chieko would return soon.

The eastern part of Hiroshima burned continuously and the sky above it was blood red. We could see it from our garden now since most of the buildings and trees were destroyed and nothing was left to block our view. Bedtime for children had passed a long time ago but my cousin Yoshi and I couldn't sleep at all. Since we were told not to leave the house, we continued with our games in the playroom.

It wasn't until after midnight, that my father came home. "Everyone alright?" Mother heard him shouting and ran towards his voice. She found him collapsed in the front doorway. He wasn't moving. Sweeping up the shattered glass throughout the bedroom, Mother found the most even surface she could, laid out a futon and dragged father's immobile body and put him into bed.

"Your father was heavy! It was brute strength that allowed me to move him that day," she told me later. "I think I did pretty well on my own!" My Mom was about the size of an eleven-year-old Westerner.

Over the next few days my father, bedridden, continued to moan and suffer from diarrhoea, nausea, and the pain from his injuries. Burned by radiation from outside his internal organs were affected as well. He couldn't consume solid food. He only survived on water and thinned rice congee. My mother borrowed a wagon from a farmer and spread a straw mat on it and placed Dad on the wagon. She pushed him to Furuta National Elementary School in hope of finding a doctor.

Mushroom cloud from the bomb dropped on Hiroshima
credit Hiroshima Peace Memorial Museum

This poem was written in 1945 by Yuzuko Kanamoto, an eight-year-old schoolmate of mine.

Beneath the Mushroom Cloud
"Ka-Boom!"
The rain came pouring down.
My mother gave me a piggy-back,
and we escaped into the mountains.
After a while we returned home.
All the people that passed in front of the
house were like ghosts.
They came to us asking for "water, water!"
Mother gave everyone some.

Shinichi's tricycle - credit Hiroshima Peace Memorial Museum

Three-year-old Shinichi died in the bomb blast while riding his tricycle. His father wanted to keep him close by and buried him and his trike in the back yard. Forty years later, his father transferred his son's remains to the family grave and donated his tricycle to the Peace Memorial Museum.

Hospital Casualties

Furuta National Elementary School became a refuge where the injured as well as those escaping the city came to drop down on mats and sleep. Emergency doctors and nurses were there to tend to the casualties. The Furuta National School was located on the west side of Hiroshima City. The school was surrounded by a little mountain, which protected it from the blast. Luckily there were no fires in this district. So many people who had been fleeing from Hiroshima city headed west to escape the fire. As well as the school, there was a community hall, a shrine, and a temple that became shelters for those evacuated from the city. All the air raid shelters were filled with children and elders. Along the mountainside, one side of the road was filled with injured people dragging their bodies towards the shelters, while on the other side, some were heading back to the city to find lost families and friends.

My mother desperately wanted my father to be examined by a doctor. Every day, under the blazing sun, she pulled the wagon to the school hoping her turn would come to see a doctor. With each passing day, the number of casualties increased. Eventually she had to give up.

For a week my father hadn't been able to get up from his bed. He had no visible injuries on the surface of his body but radiation had spread inside his body. Though he was suffering from his illness, he told us what had happened the moment the atomic bomb was dropped on Hiroshima city.

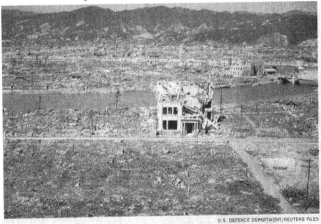

Hiroshima after the bomb

The Story of my Father

My father was at his work desk reading some documents when he saw the flash of light. He awoke to find himself covered by a pile of debris. He didn't know how long he had been unconscious. He looked around. No one was there. He called his colleagues' names.

No answer. No sound. Silence. He was buried in rubbish and dust. There was a plank of wood on his chest pinning him down. He couldn't move at all. He thought a bomb had dropped in his office and everyone had escaped except him. Fortunately both his hands were free and he started removing the debris. But the thick piece of wood was too heavy to move. He couldn't get out of his chair.

'What can I do?' he thought. He looked around for a way to escape and noticed a saw lying among the debris. He reached for it but it was too far. He spotted a long thin pole lying close to him. Using the pole he managed to pull the saw towards him. 'With the saw I can cut this heavy wood and get it off my body,' he decided. It was difficult to saw without changing his position. He struggled with all his strength, using both hands, back and forth, back and forth to slowly whittle away at the heavy piece of wood weighing down on his chest. The effort of cutting made him tired. 'I wonder why, I feel so tired. I am a strong man.' He felt so hot. He looked behind him. There was a fire with flames burning briskly. In a panic, he didn't remember how he had done it, but he quickly escaped from his office.

"If it was five minutes later, I would be dead," he said.

Downtown Hiroshima was completely demolished. Wounded people were running about in confusion, going this way and that. One of them said, "This way is better, there is fire ahead of us, go toward the river!"

While we were running forward, suddenly flames shot up.

"Let's go back this way."

"No, No. It's the wrong way."

There was agonizing crying, confusion, and people moving about aimlessly.

"Please save this child!" a woman holding a bleeding child begged him.

"Take me home," pleaded someone who had lost a leg.

"Please look after this little child," said another. "She is hungry, please give her some food! Help! Help!"

But my father said he could tell that child was already dead. "I wished I could help them, but I was barely able to support myself. I often felt I would faint while I was walking." "Be patient. I will tell a rescuer your child needs help. I am sorry. Please wait. I will find a helper," he said. "These words were no comfort to them under the circumstances, but I had no way to help them. Suddenly a man stood up and cried out to the air,"

"*Tennou heika banzai,*" literally saying, "Glory to the Emperor!" Then, he collapsed and died.

My father said the ground was covered with men and women on top of each other. "There was no road on which to even place one foot in front of the other. I stepped over piled-up corpses for miles and miles all the way home. It was like a burning hell."

His voice was getting weak but still he was talking to us.

"I wondered if I was dreaming or not. No, no, it wasn't a dream. It was happening in this world. I was a lucky man to be able to come back home to my family."

There were thousands of people suffering from their injuries. Some were too tired to walk. "I couldn't believe it. There were so many blackened, dead bodies all over the ground, not only humans but animals too. They were tangled all over the road. We couldn't find any bare patches at all."

My father was so ill. He was poisoned by the radiation and couldn't eat and had diarrhoea. Day by day he lost his energy. He couldn't get out of his bed.

On August 15th 1945, Japan surrendered. The Emperor made a public broadcast, announcing that the war was over. When Dad heard the Emperor's announcement, he said, "What a good day. How wonderful! From now on we will have a peaceful future. Go to the backyard where you will see a little mound, and dig in the soil."

There we found a plentiful supply of foods like rice, wheat, sugar, salt, miso, soy sauce and beans that my father had hidden for us. Also there was a safety box. Inside, there was enough money, stocks and bonds to support the Shindo family. These food supplies were a great help during such a time of shortages. Unfortunately shortly after, the government changed the money and it was no longer worth anything. The currency of Japanese yen had changed into New Yen, the value of the old money dropped so much it was like waste paper. My mother, who had never worked, would soon begin her harsh existence as a war widow.

Takasu Park

August 16th 1945, ten days after the bomb exploded, also one day after Japan's unconditional surrender to the United States of America, our family lost its father.

It was a sunny, sweltering hot day again. In the ten-mat-tatami room, there was the household Buddhist altar. My father's body was set in front of this altar covered by a piece of white sheet, and his face was covered with a white cloth. The droning of cicadas seemed to make the hot summer day even hotter.

About twenty people were sitting around my father's body. The monk arrived. He was wearing an official black kimono uniform. He approached my father's body and seated himself in front of the white sheet covering my father. He gave a deep bow saying, *"Namuamidabutsu."* Then he went to the household Buddhist altar and began burning incense. He took the Sutra and started reciting. The ten-tatami-mat room was quiet except for his low voice. Everyone sat respectfully listening to his incantations. After the prayer, the monk gave a sermon. I don't remember what he said. It was rather boring. The ladies of the neighbourhood gathered together and served a cup of tea, paste of sweet potatoes, figs, and watermelons.

In Takasu Park, many holes had been dug, into which dead bodies could be placed and cremated. The size of each hole was just large enough for a body. In the hole, pieces of wood were lined up horizontally and evenly. After my father's funeral in my home, his body was carried by a farmer's carriage to Takasu Park. His body was placed on top of a futon mat and covered with a new white sheet. I watched four workers with bandanas around their heads lower my father's body into the hole.

My family and some neighbours were standing a short distance from the hole staring at it. At the final service the monk recited a short sutra and prayer.

"*Namuamidabutsu, Namuamidabutsu*," all the attendants chanted.

Then a workman piled some twigs on top of my father's body and poured gasoline from a bottle onto it. Suddenly the flames flew high up the air.

"No, No! Don't burn my father." I dashed toward him but was caught by someone and brought back to my mother.

Everyone started moaning. The fire consuming my father's body burned briskly. Flames from other graves burned around us. The entire park was turned to a crematory. The smell of burning dead bodies was terrible. You could hardly breathe. But no one complained. I felt like vomiting. I glanced at my cousin Yoshi. He was standing still, watching the fire.

My Dear Cousin, Yoshi, and Aunt Chieko

My cousin Yoshi was only three and a half when the bomb was dropped. While his father was off fighting in the war, his mother brought Yoshi back to her hometown to live with my family. At the height of the war, everyone, including women, participated in whatever way he or she could. Many worked in the ammunition factory. My mother and the ladies in her neighbourhood had been assigned to volunteer at the factory downtown on August 6th. My mother had a five-month old baby. Yoshi's mother, Aunt Chieko, told my Mom, "You shouldn't be taking the baby downtown through all the pollution. Besides, you'll be busy nursing. Let me go in your place. Just look after Yoshi for me." And so my Aunt Chieko met her unjust fate and died when the bomb dropped.

For days afterwards Mother was in a crazed state, after trying and failing to get medical help for my father, she would ask my grandmother to look after the infant and my sick father, and she would spend hours on end combing the city, looking for any clues of Aunt Chieko. The city was covered in ashes, still smoldering with pockets of fire. The blazing hot summer sun baked the human and animal carcasses that lay everywhere. There were maggots all over them. The odour of rotting corpses was suffocating. Flies swarmed around as the crows and ravens were picking away at the remains of human and animal flesh.

My mother finally received some information from a neighbour who had been evacuated to the community hall. Aunt Chieko's group had headed east. My mother held on tightly to this bit of hope and continued her search. All she encountered were rescue workers silenced by exhaustion. She spent days searching through a city of living hell. Those scenes, and the guilt that Aunt Chieko had gone in her place, continued to trouble her for the rest of her life.

It is said that mothers have unrelenting strength. She was so busy taking my father to see the doctor, searching for Aunt Chieko while nursing the baby Yuta, preparing family meals and looking after us kids. She worked non-stop with little time to sleep. Despite all her efforts, my mother could not find any trace of Aunt Chieko. Her remains, clothes and personal articles seemed to have been incinerated. Now, Aunt Chieko is remembered in Hiroshima's Peace Park at the monument to shelter the souls of the victims of the atomic bomb. Not only did Yoshi lose his mother, his father never returned from the war, so Yoshi became an orphan. He lived with us for a while, until he was adopted into the family of another aunt, Keiko who had four daughters but no sons to carry on the family lineage. Although my mother felt an unconditional commitment and desire to take a lifelong responsibility to raise Yoshi, at the Shindo family, a gathering of all the other relatives, they decided that it would be best for Yoshi to live with Chieko's sister, Aunt Keiko.

The following poem was written by Yoshi when he was ten years old. It appears in "Beneath the Mushroom Cloud," and was published in 1952 by Aoki Shoten. The first time I read this poem it left such a deep impression on me that I can never forget.

Mother Vanished

A Sad Memory
Each time I see my friends'
Fathers and Mothers
I can't help but think
If there hadn't been a war
If there hadn't been a war
How happy I would be
Father on the right side
Mother on the left side
But my father was killed
in a far away battle
My gentle, gentle mother vanished in the atomic
bomb
Only I remain all alone
No more war, I've had enough.

See appendix 1:What is an atomic bomb? What's wrong with it. Dr. Eiichio Ochiai

PART TWO

Building a New Life

What remained of the centre of the city of Hiroshima was a field of ashes. Fortunately our house wasn't completely destroyed. Although the house was tilted it was still livable and provided shelter from the rain and wind. The problem was finding food. At that time almost all commodities were rationed. We would line up at the Agricultural Cooperative Association to receive goods. The rations weren't enough for three meals a day. People constantly felt hungry. Mother went around asking the farmers up on the hillsides for anything they could spare and sometimes received gnarled and deformed pumpkins, wilted vegetables, and potatoes that would not normally be considered edible or had been nibbled at by mice.

Our backyard, which once had been a lawn, was transformed into a vegetable patch, producing a blessing of much-needed food. Among the different vegetables we grew sweet potatoes which have hearty vines and leaves. My task was to thin the leaves, and separate the young leaves and shoots which my mother would cook to eat as greens. We would eat all parts of the plant. I don't remember how they tasted.

Expeditions with my friends to the mountains and the beach often included finding goods to supplement the family's food supply. My favourite pastime was grabbing a bucket and shovel after school and heading to the beach to go clam digging with my friends. The beach was about one hour away with our small children's feet. Calculating the low tide, we shoveled away the sand and gathered clams. As high tide approached, the water rose rapidly. If we were far from the shore, we would have to race back. Mother was always thrilled to be handed a bucket full of clams.

In the late summer, amongst the weeds in the wheat fields, were green locusts. We would quietly approach a locust resting on a grass stem and attempt to capture it by cupping our hands around it. But they were wily and would often hop away just out of our reach. We needed to be skilled to catch them. We would make *tsukudani,* preserved snacks simmered in soy sauce and sugar, with these locusts. It was a crunchy and delicious treat.

There was another fun filled activity in the fall. We would go to the mountains to gather pine cones, twigs, and branches and return with bundles on our backs, to be used for fuel for our cooking stove and hot water. Fall was typhoon season in Japan. Following a typhoon we would go to the shrine that had a large gingko tree and collect the fallen gingko seeds, which contained a savoury nut, wrapped in a foul-smelling skin that often left a rash on my hands.

Most of my friends were girls, so when it rained, naturally we played house. The family structure was always as follows: father, mother, baby, and an atomic bomb victim. Yoshi was the only male, so he always played the role of Father. Using chipped rice bowls and teacups, with wild flowers and seeds as food, we substituted twigs for fish bones. We children were always hungry and when we played house we filled our empty stomachs with imaginary food. Using water we pretended to drink sake, because we were told that sake was good for atomic bomb patients. We had an alcoholic man living next door. An atomic bomb survivor, the old man had lost his hair and spent his days drinking, staggering around, and napping. Atomic bomb patients resembled modern-day chemotherapy patients. In addition to hair loss, they had rashes, a purple skin tone, and gums so weak they were constantly bleeding.

I, too, was covered in a rash. It was itchy. I always wanted to scratch it. My mother made a pair of mittens that I had to wear to prevent infection at night when I went to sleep.

Because of this rash, my mother would prepare special white rice for me. Even though the rice was rare and expensive she got that treat as soy products were believed not to be good for the rash. The rest of the family had to eat soybeans.

The west side of Hiroshima where we were living in the Takasu district was not damaged like downtown Hiroshima. From the burning and completely demolished downtown, many refugees were still coming toward the west side of Hiroshima's suburbs. Among them, orphans and old people with dirty faces wearing raggedy clothes. I was so sorry to see them and wanted to give them some food.

In the kitchen, there was a cookie jar on the top of the shelf that I couldn't reach. I bet that the cookies were kept there intentionally to save for a special occasion.

I brought a chair, reached the jar and snuck some cookies into my pocket. Then I rushed out of the house and went to the road where those people were passing by. I sat down beside the road and waited to hand out the cookies to those people. This charity was continued until my mother noticed there were fewer and fewer cookies. Mother was very angry, and I was in big trouble. That night, I couldn't sleep. In my mind there were many pitiful people passing by my house.

'What can I do? How can I help those people?' I was thinking as I lay in bed.

'I want to build a big house, and we can all live together. One room is for this girl, one room is for the old lady, and another room is…. Oh, there are so many, I have to build a mansion for them, so we can all fit in.'

I kept my dream for a long time that one day I would find a peaceful house where it would be like heaven. In this heaven, there would be peace and harmony. No one would fight, no war. There would be plenty of food and water. No pain, no tears, no suffering, no struggle. Also, those who live in this heaven would have eternal happy life. Everyone, let's go there!

My Mother Misao

Misao became a widow when she was 30 years old. Since my father's death, it was up to her alone to support her family — my grandmother, my little brother, and me. She had never experienced working outside the home and had never worked for money in her life. But now she had to do something for a living. Luckily we had a big home that she could use as a boardinghouse. She boarded four Hiroshima University students in the house and was busy cooking and washing their clothes every day. I always thought she never rested but she was healthy.

When I was in Grade 6, my mother's health started to decline. She often lay down in bed. My mother's mother, my grandma came from Hagi City to help us. But one day Grandma had a stroke and she became paralyzed. We were all at a loss as to what to do. All the students left our home and we had to move to my mother's hometown, Hagi City, located in the next prefecture to Hiroshima. We rented our Takasu house instead of selling it. I was in Grade 9 and my brother was in Grade 1.

My Brother Yuta

Yuta was only five months old when the atomic bomb exploded in Hiroshima.

Even during the time of food shortage, he drank mother's milk and was a glowing healthy, chubby baby. His cheeks were fat and round like a red apple. They almost covered his nose. He never remembered our father because he was so young when Dad died.

Yuta was a very active little boy who played in a field or in the little stream in front of our house catching fish and tadpoles all day long. His clothes were always muddy and every single day Mother or I had to wash them. We were eight years apart so as a big sister I had to take care of him. When we fought, Yuta teased me and then quickly escaped. When he got mad at me, he often wiggled his nose. So I nicknamed him "little piggy." He was good at showing tricks to his friends. He managed to learn new tricks from the neighbour who was in bed, ill from the atomic bomb's effects. Maybe Yuta's visits to this poor man comforted him. Sometimes Yuta got some snacks and fruits from him. He always brought them back home in wrapped paper and shared them with me. He was naughty, but on the other hand, he was a very tender boy.

We sometimes visited the junkyard. We searched for some broken items to bring back home. There were no toys to play with in those days so pieces of junk became our toys. Yuta had a treasure box where he kept some metal pieces. On rainy days he opened the treasure box and played with these discarded items making interesting objects and had named each one of them. But for me, they were still just junk.

When he was eighteen years old, he graduated from his high school in Hagi and went to university in Nagoya where he lived in a dormitory. He studied electronics, became an engineer and worked in this occupation until he retired.

Time went by and he developed stomach cancer when he was in his forties, but luckily recovered and still lives in Hiroshima with his wife, two daughters, and four grandchildren. He is one of the baby survivors of the atomic bomb and gets some medical support from Hiroshima City, as do all survivors.

My Grandmother, Chizu

My father Kazuo and Auntie Chieko were brother and sister. Their mother Chizu, my grandmother, was a very faithful and diligent Buddhist. She was always in front of the Buddha altar when she found time, praying and reciting *"Namu-amida-butsu,"* paying homage to Buddha.

She had her own little house like a tearoom across from our house. It was reached by crossing a footbridge. She lived there alone but when mealtime came, she ate with us. We crossed the bridge to go to her little house. In her room was a Buddha's altar where incense was burned constantly, so her little house smelled like incense. She frequently made offerings of fruits or pieces of Japanese cake and cookies at her altar to Buddha. When I visited her, she would go to the altar and bow once with both hands together and say, *"Namu-amida-butsu."* Then she took these offerings down and gave them to me. The cookies smelt like incense but still tasted good. I was so pleased to have them. She sometimes told me a story of Heaven and Hell. There were even pictures of them in her room.

One evening, my grandma called me. "Sa-chi, Sa-chi. Come here. Come. Hurry up."

I pretended not to hear her voice because I was playing an interesting game. Also, it was bath time. After a while I went to see my Grandma and she said, "Oh, too bad, you didn't come when I called you. There were beautiful angels lined up and heading toward the western sky where Heaven is. There was a gorgeous wagon in the sky. I bet there was someone in it. Too bad you missed seeing it."

Oh, how disappointed I was. I imagined my father was inside the wagon on his way to Heaven! I still recall that day. Grandma Chizu died at the age of 75 in the summer, just around the time of the Obon Festival when Buddhists believe the spirits of their ancestors are returning to the earth.

Grandma Chizu and Sachi

Aunt Hisako My Birth Mother

After I graduated from Furuta Elementary School, I started going to Hiroshima Mission Women's Junior High School. My Aunt Hisako and her son, Jiyo and daughter, Toshi lived close to the school. Hisako's eldest son, Fujihiko, had been hospitalized with tuberculosis. Aunt Hisako was a very modern woman. She spoke good English and worked at the American base as a typist. Her nickname at the base was Martha. She wore stylish dresses and smoked cigarettes. I hadn't seen a woman smoking in my life. So, to me, she was an exciting lady instead of my aunt. She sometimes invited me to her home after school, or she visited on holidays in my Takasu home. Aunt Hisako was very kind to me. One day she made matching dresses for Toshi and me. The dresses were frilly with lots of pretty flowers in the fabric. Aunt Hisako took us to a photo studio to have our photos taken together. Toshi and I were cousins and day-by-day we became just like sisters.

My mother Misao had been ill for three years. When I was in Grade 9, Misao decided to move back to her hometown where she could get help from her brothers and sisters.

One day, Aunt Hisako asked me if I would live with her family instead of moving to Hagi as my school was very close to her house. If I moved how could I bring relief to my household? Who was going to look after my sick mother Misao and little Yuta? Toshi's big brother, Jiyo, sent me an invitation letter saying to come and live with them. "You are most welcome." The letter was very tempting to my heart, but it felt wrong to leave my sick mom and little Yuta. It was early spring; I went out to my garden and read the letter many times and was wondering what to do. I walked around in circles in the garden trying to make a decision by myself. Finally I showed my mother the letter from Jiyo and told my mother that Aunt Hisako asked me to move to her home instead of going to Hagi.

Misao mother was quiet for a while then

said, "Listen, Sachi. It was your father's wish not to tell you the truth, that you were adopted into our Shindo family by Aunt Hisako. Your father even registered at city hall that you, Sachi, were the first child of the Shindo family. It was a false registration but he made it on purpose," she continued. "I can't hide this story from you any longer. It is time to tell you the truth and especially now that your birth mother is asking you to live with her. You better consider seriously but without stressing too much. You decide what is best for you. Don't worry about us."

I was at a loss. I was so shocked to learn that my Shindo father was not my real father. I just couldn't accept the fact. NO way! He died from the atomic bomb explosion. Nevertheless, he still lived in my heart. Was Aunt Hisako my real mother and Jiyo and Toshi my brother and sister? I couldn't believe it. The news shocked me so much I was unable to get out of bed for two weeks. It was a hard decision but I really had to make up my mind. Finally, I decided to move to Hagi with Misao mother and little Yuta.

Aunt Hisako came to say goodbye just

before we were going to Hagi. Misao told me to go to the train station with Aunt Hisako to say goodbye. We walked together hand in hand to the train station. There was no one at the tiny platform with one bench. Aunt Hisako turned to me and asked, "Sachi, would you call me mother?" I was silent. She said again. "Sachi, I am your mother, please call me mother. Only once is enough." Aunt Hisako's eyes started tearing. I was still silent. I could not say so. I could see a long curved train track in the far distance but no train was coming. I stood beside Aunt Hisako and wished that a train would come soon. I just wanted to be a Shindo's daughter.

My Birth Father

My birth father, Haruki Komura, was an earnest Buddhist. He dedicated his life to preaching Buddhism in Japan. Unfortunately he had tuberculosis and stayed in a sanatorium for several years. He wrote his autobiography called "Look Up To The Light." In this book the first chapter is dedicated, "To my beloved wife Hisako."

Since I started to preach Buddhism, I became so poor and lost my health. I felt sorry for you that you were raising three children as well as looking after me and working as a typist. You were earning our daily expenses and you were supporting me. Many thanks Hisako. Nevertheless, I was eager to seek after truth and I spent all of my money for this search. People think this was a waste of time and my life was rusty but I denied it. During the three years of my sickness I gained patience, instead of an arrogant mind. Complaint turned to compliance. I can accept everything now. My inner soul has grown happy. I hope you are happy about this. When I regain my health in another few years, I want you to travel with me and preach Buddhism. I will never be rich because my soul cannot accept an easy life. I hope you can understand me, being my wife.

His life had been stoic and dedicated to volunteer work. I never met him because I was adopted into my aunt's home. But when I read his book, I felt very close to him. It seems we are connected in spirit even if he was Buddhist and I am now a Christian.

The House that a Raccoon Entered

Our new house in Hagi stood behind a stone sake warehouse. It was once used to distill sake but was closed during the Second World War. It had a large room with one small window set in the stone wall at the east side. The entrance door was made of wood and had a small window on top; these two windows provided sufficient light for the room. In a corner of the warehouse was a wooden kitchen, built to avoid rain and snow. In another corner of the room was a small washroom.

This was our new house where my mother, Misao, my little brother, Yuta and I settled down to live. My mother had a wooden bed in the corner of the room where she spent most of the day. I don't know what kind of sickness she had. I think partly it was stress from the shock of the atomic bomb. They called it "dangling sickness." She had no energy. She just stayed in bed or moped around the place. Yuta and I slept on the tatami mats with futon mattresses and covers. It was a cozy room for the three of us together.

During the daytime we put away all our futons and used the table both for dining and as a study desk. One Japanese room changes instantly from a bedroom to a living room, a dining room, a study and even a playroom. Isn't it magic? We used the bath in the main house and my aunt often cooked some food for us.

One night while we were sleeping, we were awoken by a big bang. We turned on the light. A raccoon was crouching in the corner of the dressers. I was so scared of animals. I asked Yuta to chase away the raccoon with a broom. Poor raccoon, he was terribly scared of us and ran about our small room. Yuta chased the raccoon for a while until it finally went out. What a strange thing to happen. The raccoon entered from the hole in the wood door that we had temporarily patched with a piece of newspaper. The raccoon ripped through the paper and got into the room. I bet he had smelt some delicious leftover food. Despite this intrusion, we still had a nice house compared to

Hiroshima's temporary shelters.

It was now 1955, ten years after the bomb. Hiroshima was still in the process of restoration. Large institutions, government offices, main stores in the downtown were starting to be rebuilt. But the majority of the victims from the atomic bomb were still struggling. In the burned city, there were scattered shacks, barracks, and temporary shelters. Some huts were just made of scrap wood, covered with tinplate sheets to avoid rain. When the rain started the tinplate roofs rattled noisily and water started leaking into the shelters. In wintertime the snow fell down around the shacks. People had to stuff the doors and window crevices with papers and rags to keep out cold draughts. Their deformed kitchen utensils had been scrounged from the city ruins. They had to fetch water from the nearest well. These shelters were more like temporary campsites than permanent homes.

Many homeless people lived in this disastrous, ruined town along with orphans whose families had been killed by the atomic bomb. These people were usually helping each other but sometimes had small quarrels amongst themselves due their difficult lives. One boy, whose face was like a monster from the atomic bomb burn, became the boss among the orphans. His face was his weapon of intimidation to all other orphans who had to obey him. What a pity to use his deformed face as a way of survival. But this was the reality at that time.

It was said that in the city of Hiroshima neither trees nor flowers would grow for another seventy years. But the next year a tree with reddish flowers called a rosebay started growing. This was the first tree growing in the ruined city of Hiroshima. Some years later, one of the burnt-out paulownia trees started to grow fresh shoots. It grew into a large tree and is located in the Hiroshima Memorial Peace Park.

Hagi city was never damaged by the war and is known as a castle town. It was an ancient historical city of Japan, like Kyoto and Nagoya. When I was fifteen, my mother, Misao and six-year-old brother Yuta spent four years there. As the years went by, I was happy to see that my mother recovered from her sickness. When I was in Grade 11, she found a job as a janitor in a small branch of an insurance company. She never had work experience in her life and was thrilled to find this job. She was a very diligent and elegant worker. The office staff called her, "a peacock among crows." My mother started her new life when she was in her forties. She loved her job and always said, "All the staff are so kind to me, I am very happy to work there."

I respected her and was very proud of my beautiful mother, Misao.

My step-mother Misao, me, and my brother Yuta

Home Coming

After graduation from Hagi High School, my mother, Misao, my brother, Yuta and I moved back to Hiroshima. I found a job at the Hiroshima Bank. Blue jackets with white shirts were the colours of our bank uniform. Thirty of us worked together in one big room and each section was divided into groups of desks with about six chairs. I was one of the receptionists. The first time I had to say, "Welcome Sir or Madam," to each client, my voice was small and trembling. I was very shy about having to sit down facing the entrance.

My co-worker, Mika had been working more than five years in various sections of the bank. She had confidence and experience and supported me a lot. She was a hard worker and a cheerful lady who swished rapidly among desks just like a little mouse running through the cornfields.

But she sometimes became weak and had to

rest in a corner of the staffroom. One day at lunchtime she showed me her arm covered with purple spots and told me her story of survival from the atomic bomb. "Look, when these spots appear on my body, it is a reaction to the nuclear radiation. I feel no energy and have to rest." And she started to tell me her story:

On August 6th, I was working in a factory called, 'a labour service corps.' All the high school students were sent to some factory or place downtown to work for Hiroshima City because the majority of men had gone off to war. Due to the labour shortage in Japan, there was no one to teach classes at school. There were no holidays, even on Sunday. We worked seven days a week. We high school students were wearing white bandanas that had written in black ink, "hissho," meaning "certain victory." All Japanese were brainwashed into believing that we would surely win the Second World War.

Mika's class was divided into two groups. One group went to Hiroshima city to work in a military factory making weapons. Others, like Mika, were sent to the suburbs near an area called Takasu near my home. Luckily, Mika's life was saved because she was in Takasu. Most of the other students who were working in a downtown factory died instantly when the atomic bomb exploded. Mika was injured by broken glass. She didn't want to say anything about being a lucky person who didn't die. She felt so sorry for her classmates who died that day, and guilty for having survived.

Arranged Marriage

When I turned twenty-two, my mother asked me to meet a man who was looking for a bride. In Japan, in those days, a so-called "matchmaker" or "go between" arranged the majority of marriages.

The system was as follows: At first you prepared your handwritten resume. It included your family tree, your education, your hobbies and the best possible photo of yourself — usually we went to a photo studio to take a formal picture in a Kimono. In the case of a man, he would wear a dark suit. Then the matchmaker would take the photos and resume to a young member of the opposite sex who was looking for a potential partner to marry. Your family would examine the resume and photo and discuss if this person was suitable or not for you. If you agreed, the matchmaker arranged for you to meet each other. Usually the meeting place was at a fancy hotel restaurant. You greeted each other and had a cup of tea or coffee with cake.

Then the matchmaker asked,

"Would you like to be together for a while and sit down around the lobby, or go to the garden to talk to each other?"

If both of you were interested to find out more about each other, you'd go together and chat for a while. Then you'd part.

Later, both the girl and the boy would let the matchmaker know what their impressions were and if they wanted to meet again or not. If so, the matchmaker left them alone for their second date. If they liked one another, the couple decided to marry. It depended on their will. Sometimes, this traditional arranged meeting still continues today, but in those days it was the custom.

Following this method, I wrote my resume carefully and neatly and handed it to the matchmaker, Mrs. Wada. Among several men, she selected one gentleman and arranged our first date at a hotel lobby. I wore a beautiful dress with a pearl necklace and high-heel shoes and went to this hotel lobby. I was so tense; my heart was trembling to meet this gentleman. The matchmaker said to me, "Sachi, relax and ask him some questions. Find out what kind of person he is, but don't talk too much. A quiet girl is a good sign."

My handicap was that I had been raised by a single mother after my father died. My education history was only that of a high school graduate. On top of that I was a survivor of the atomic bomb. Even so, he wanted to continue to date me. My mother said, "He is such a fine man. You keep going with him." He had a high level of education and a good government job. His was twenty-nine years old. One month later, he wanted to arrange our engagement. I wasn't ready so soon but my mother said, "After you are engaged to him you will feel a more sincere love toward him." I didn't have any experience of love so I thought I should obey my mother. We were engaged on January 20th, which is my birthday. One day he said that he was not interested in material things except books. He loved books. "So don't worry about preparing the bride's furniture and house items." Traditionally, a bride brings all the furniture to their new home. The groom gives some money to his future bride when they are engaged.

We met each other once a week but I still didn't feel love toward him. Our wedding date was set for May. What could I do? I couldn't marry him without love. I had to make up my mind soon. Everyone was congratulating us on our engagement especially my mother. One day I met him and I told him my honest feeling that I didn't love him yet. I wanted to postpone our wedding ceremony. He agreed, but some official documentation had to be submitted before our marriage. This was too stressful for me so finally I told the matchmaker to forget about our getting engaged. This caused a lot of trouble. My mother and his family were really angry. We compensated him, and returned the money he had spent on an engagement ring, the dating fee, and compensation for his mental anguish.

From the start, I felt this marriage arrangement was being rushed. Everyone, except me, was really pushy. Maybe, because he was nearly thirty years old he was anxious to marry soon but I, on the other hand, was not ready to move forward so quickly. It was a very uncomfortable experience for me. I didn't want to think of it and didn't care if I ever married. I felt freedom.

Lost Love

In 1962, I moved to Tokyo where my birth mother, Hisako, two brothers and sister were living. I was suddenly part of a big family for me compared to my Hiroshima Shindo family. But soon after, one brother, Jiyo moved to work at the Atomic Energy Research Center in Mito, and my sister, Toshiko married and moved out. I was receiving unemployment insurance money and started taking an English Conversation course. My English was so poor. One day I was on a train. There was a tall, chubby foreigner standing beside me. Suddenly he said some words to me. I couldn't understand him at all. Many passengers looked toward us. I was embarrassed not being able to reply to him. Why had he asked *me*? There were many other passengers on the train. My face became red. When the next station came, I got off the train and sat on a bench to cool off my face and still my heart. I realized that Tokyo is a big city where people gathered from different parts of the country and from around the world. I needed to polish up my English. So I started to study basic English.

Meanwhile, my brother Jiyo introduced me to his friend who had been living in Tokyo. We started dating and he tutored me in English when he had time. Gradually we became boyfriend and girlfriend. He was a tall and well-muscled man. I was short and slim.

We went to see movies, spent time chatting in cafés, and had trips to the beach just like any couple. I liked him a lot. But unfortunately a parting day came. As we sat in the corner of a coffee shop, he whispered, "Sachi, sorry but my mother is against our relationship. The reason is because you are the survivor of the atomic bomb." I just listened. "I feel sorrow toward you and am unhappy with my mother. There is no evidence saying that your body is healthy or not." We didn't talk too much, just said goodbye to our love.

When I came home, I sat down at the table alone and my tears spilled out endlessly. I sobbed until the room had become dark with nightfall. Later my boyfriend told my brother, "Sorry, but I couldn't convince my mom. Your sister is lovely and I respect her."

At that time there were rumours saying the effects of the atomic bomb would be contagious. No clear evidence was available that could prove or deny it. The atomic bomb destroyed human lives, left deep painful scars on people's bodies and hearts. It also pushed away pure love. I heard many stories from women and men who were rejected because they were the survivors of the atomic bomb. The social stigma of a reaction toward the atomic bomb survivors was understandable. This was the first occurrence in history of an atomic bomb being dropped on a city. There was no data or evidence showing the long-term effects. Even today, I think, there remains many unknown and undiscovered effects from nuclear radiation, both on the earth and on humans.

Atomic Bomb Maidens

After the Second World War there were many young female victims known as "atomic bomb maidens." Those young girls who were in the prime of their youth quietly secluded themselves at home and refused to go out in public. Their bodies were scarred and their facial features disfigured by the fires that had followed the blast. With "keloid scars" they were permanently wounded in both mind and body.

Norman Cousins (1915-1990), a journalist and writer, visited Japan in 1949. Witnessing a vast number of orphans – many wounded, he started to support those atomic bomb maidens. Norman, together with Pastor Taniguchi of Hiroshima Nagarekawa Church, established an adoption organization, "The Spirit Adoption Movement." Norman collected $50,000 in donations from American citizens. He invited twenty-five atomic bomb maidens to New York's Mt. Sinai Hospital to undergo plastic surgery operations to remake their disfigured faces and remove their keloid scars.

Unfortunately, one girl died during surgery. The next day, girls lying in the operating room courageously agreed that their treatment proceed. The operation transplanted skin from the abdomen and thigh. Some girls' surgery was repeated several times to accomplish a satisfactory result. After the successful surgery one maiden was so happy to find that her fingers were no longer sticking together. They were separated and she could wiggle each finger and use chopsticks again. Another said after the operation, "I can open my mouth wide and laugh."

Another maiden exclaimed, "I no longer have to cover up my arm. Look! No more scars."

During their stay in America, the home-stay families were so kind and treated them as members of their family. The young women said that Americans were really kind and warm-hearted people. They had saved them from the horror of darkness and had given them back their lives. The women learned how to laugh and enjoy life again. Among twenty-four maidens, some were returned to Hiroshima, some remained in America and were adopted by American families or married Americans. Surely they were lucky people to get those surgeries and regain their confidence to live with open minds. But the majority of the survivors who were damaged both in body and mind from the atomic bomb continued to live in a corner of their homes secluded from their families and society. It is beyond imagination how lonely their lives were.

This is a poem of a mother whose daughter was injured from the atomic bomb.

Aware Aware ikutose heteha kieusen
Hanako no kubi no keroido no iro.
How pitiful, how pitiful,
Hanako's scar of Keloid.
It will never disappear from her neck.

PART THREE

Gaijin
How I Met My Husband,
Charles Rummel

"Gaijin" - This is a typical nickname the Japanese use when referring to Caucasian or white foreigners regardless of their country of origin. The majority of foreigners in Japan at that time were American Army personnel from the military bases of Yokosuka, Atsugi, Tachikawa, or Yokote, which were close to Tokyo.

In 1962, on a very cold day in January, I met a Canadian, Charles Rummel who had come to

Tokyo as an exchange student. We were at St. Louis Café in Kanda. A group of us had gathered there for an English Conversation circle organized by Hawaiian-born Mac Yokoi, our English teacher. Charles was brought along as Mac's guest.

When I saw him the first time, my recollection was that he had big green eyes in a deep forehead. His eyes were like marbles. He introduced himself to everyone. "My name is Chuck. Chuck, as in Y.K.K. zipper." He imitated pulling his jacket zipper up and down. In Japanese, the word for zipper is "chuck." We all laughed at his humour. On the way home, I was behind him walking along the narrow road with my friends. Chuck was taking a pair of gloves out of his jacket's pocket and accidentally dropped a 1000 yen note on the road. I picked it up and handed it to him. He thanked me, then we walked to the train station together. We had to go in the same direction to return to our homes so we got a train together and sat down, my friend, myself, and Chuck. I was in the middle. When the transfer station came, saying "good bye," he jokingly wiped a tear with a piece of tissue and put it in his pocket. At that time I could never imagine that Chuck would end up being my husband. Since that chance meeting, many things happened just by luck between Chuck and me.

In April, his parents were sailing to Japan aboard a Shinnihon Steamship Company vessel. I was working for this company as a typist. So Chuck phoned me to find out the date of the ship's arrival and which port it would be entering. Because this was a cargo vessel its destination wouldn't be decided until the last minute. Chuck and I talked on the phone several times about this matter. When their boat arrived, I went to Yokohama pier with Chuck to welcome his parents. They started sightseeing around Japan and I was invited to join them, or maybe it was just Chuck who decided to have me join these excursions. I don't know. I wondered what his parents thought about me. I could hardly speak English and I was not Chuck's girlfriend — just a friend. I was a mysterious little girl to them, coming, and guiding them around Tokyo, Nikko, Kamakura. Actually, Chuck knew these areas better than I did.

One day Chuck invited me to go to a party being held at the Canadian Embassy. I went to this party where I met Mr. and Mrs. Forrester who were Chuck's neighbours in West Vancouver and happened to be friends of my brother who was studying at Tokyo University.

Chuck and I started dating. At the beginning, we both had a hard time recognizing each other. To Chuck, all Japanese girls appeared identical. To me, all foreigners looked the same. Tokyo is one of the busiest cities in the world. Our meeting place was Yuraku-cho, in front of the Sanai building, which was a popular place for many people to meet each other. I judged him by the jacket he wore every time we met. Sometimes we waited for 30 minutes although we were standing close to each other. Once, we were standing back to back.

Once in a while I invited him to my home and he had dinner with my family. When he ate a piece of bread he put plenty of butter on it. My mother complained, "Whenever Chuck comes our butter disappears quickly." Butter was expensive in Japan. Chuck told me in Canada, there was a lot of butter, cheese, milk, and meat. I envied his country but, in my mind, Canada was a part of America. Later I found out Canada was an independent country. As an atomic bomb survivor, my dubious feelings toward him were released and I felt happy he wasn't American. We often went hiking with other couples in the suburbs of Tokyo. When picnic days came, I got up early and was happy to make lunch for us.

Summer came. It was time for Chuck to go back to Canada, to his hometown of Vancouver. He was leaving by cargo boat from Yokohama pier. It was a beautiful day in 1962. Several of his friends and students from the high school, where he'd taught English, came to say goodbye to him. He seemed very happy talking with them. I hesitated going too close to him so I was standing behind these crowds. Then the final bell rang. There were many people on the pier waiting for the boat to leave. Chuck ran up the steps of the boat. The farewell music started. There were colorful tapes tied up between those seeing people off and those leaving

"Good bye!" "Sayonara!" People were crying and shouting loudly. Suddenly, a white tape was thrown in front of me. I caught it. Chuck had thrown it to me. Music continued. Yokohama pier had a nice breeze with colorful tapes dangling and swaying. Chuck was busy from the deck moving to right and left to control our white tape. The boat started heading toward the ocean. Many tapes were torn and fell off into the water. Finally, only our white tape remained in the air. The distance between the boat and the pier was increasing. The boat started going faster and faster toward the glittering sea. I tried to run faster and faster to chase the boat holding our white tape. The tape was torn from my hand. It was fluttering, twiddling as if it were dancing in the air on the blue ocean stage. People started clapping for us. After that I lost my sense of what was going on. I just kept running as Chuck's figure finally disappeared from sight.

Saying **Goodbye to Charles - 1962 - Yokohama Pier**

The Registered Cheque

On my way back home from Yokohama pier I sat on the train looking out the window. I began to feel lonely and tears ran down my cheeks. While I was dating him I felt happy and excited. Now he was far away across the ocean in Canada. I didn't think I would ever see him again. For a while I watched scenery from the window, thinking of Chuck. Then, to distract myself, I took out a book from my bag and started reading. Unable to concentrate, I read the same page again and again. The train clattered along, I stared at the passing scenery without seeing anything. Maybe my being in love with Chuck had gone with the boat, disappeared into the ocean. I recalled us both clutching white tape — him on the boat, me on the dock, until it broke. I closed my eyes.

Chuck and I started corresponding by airmail, back and forth. It usually took about two weeks for mail to reach the other side of the

Pacific Ocean. We wrote in a mixture of broken English and broken Japanese. Sometimes my friends whose major was English helped me write my letters.

One day, a registered letter came from Chuck. It said, "Please come to Vancouver and meet my family and my friends. I want you to come and see my home country, Canada. I have told you about it, now I want you to come and see it with your own eyes."

Astonishingly there was a registered cheque for $400 included in the envelope. It was a lot of money. I didn't know what to do. It was difficult for a woman to go to Canada alone without any purpose. Usually, business or exchange students were permitted to get a visa. Also the limit for taking foreign money out of Japan was $300 per person. I had long discussions with my mother and my brother about what I should do. Mom said, "Don't accept this money. But if you want to go I will pay your transportation and some living expenses while you are in Vancouver. I have been saving money for your marriage preparation. So this is it. Take responsibility for yourself while in Canada." My brother also supported me in going to Vancouver because he thought the experience of living abroad was a good education for young people. With their approval, I didn't have to think about it too much and happily decided to visit Chuck and see Canada. It took time to prepare the passport, and find a guarantor in Canada, but three months later, I found myself walking up the gangway of a large cargo ship. With my heart in my mouth, I said, "Here goes Sachi. You are walking aboard a ship which will cross the ocean to Canada."

Stepping off the boat into Vancouver

It was the spring of 1963 when I left for Canada aboard a ship owned by the company where I'd been working as a typist. It was my first time to go on an ocean voyage. Every day, we only saw the ocean and the sky. As we left Japan, seagulls swooped around the ship, then far from land, we also saw flying fish and whales. I got seasick. Since leaving Yokohama pier I stayed most of the time in my bunk, not eating but vomiting all the time. I just could not get up from my bed except to drink some tea or water. I felt I was almost dying. After a long time I could eat a little rice.

Two weeks after leaving Japan, early in the morning, the boat approached Vancouver harbour. The tall buildings of Hotel Vancouver and the high-rises stood up in the misty morning. We passed under the Lions Gate Bridge. All those buildings looked like fantasy castles. This was not Japan but Canada. I had finally arrived. Chuck, his father, his sister Dorothy, Mr. and Mrs. Forrester, and Mika Yoneda, my mother's friend, all came to welcome me. It was an unforgettable moment in my life to feel so welcomed.

The first Canadian I saw when I landed was the immigration officer. He was friendly and gave me a one-year visiting visa instead of three months. This was unexpectedly lucky for me. I gave back the cheque to Chuck, but he told me to open a bank account with the money and use it for my expenses. I was fortunate. I could homestay at Mika's home on Victoria Drive in Vancouver and start going to English school downtown.

At that time, Chuck was the owner of "Cypress Park Tea Room," in West Vancouver near his home. After his work and on Sundays he visited me, or sometimes Mika's husband, George drove me to Chuck's Tea Room when he had free time. My new life in Vancouver, Canada was very comfortable even though I didn't understand English very well. I adjusted to the western lifestyle without any resistance but I missed Japanese food.

Mika's Home

Vancouver is one of the three largest cities in Canada. I saw many Japanese Canadians, whose parents emigrated from Japan over 100 years before. During the Second World War, these first and second-generation Japanese immigrants were discriminated against. Some were sent to the war to fight, others were sent back to Japan. Most remaining Japanese Canadians were forced to move into the secluded interior countryside far from the coast. Their land, houses, cars, boats, and most of their belongings, were taken away by the Canadian Government, even for second-generation Japanese citizens born in Canada because, in World War II, Japan was fighting against Canada and United States of America.

George Yoneda`s family had been sent to Minto Village in British Columbia and he was obliged to work in the forest, cutting trees with other Japanese men. After the Second World

War, he went back to Japan and his relatives arranged for him to meet Mika, my mother's friend. At first glance, George fell in love with Mika and proposed to her immediately.

Mika also found George attractive and was excited about the idea of living in a foreign country. After their marriage, they moved to Vancouver and started a dry-cleaning business on Victoria drive. They had two little boys and were busy running their dry-cleaning business.

I went to English as a second language school all day. In the evening I often helped around the house, with dinner and babysitting.

Mika was also a survivor of the atomic bomb dropped on Hiroshima. Her house had been five kilometres away from ground zero and part of it was damaged. The windows were broken and the ceiling had fallen down. She was eleven years old and was in the classroom when the atomic bomb exploded. Her friends sitting near the windows were cut by the shattered glass and were bleeding badly. On her home, she saw some injured survivors walking away from downtown Hiroshima. It was awful so she covered her face so as not to see them as she walked home. The older students from her school had been volunteering in factories to make parts for military vessels, and weapons.

Most of those volunteer students were killed instantly by the bomb. Some survivors' ears were melted by the fire. One of them showed Mika her black pants that were burnt by the fire.

Several days after the bomb dropped, Mika went to the destroyed and burned town of Hiroshima with her mother and her little brother looking for relatives. Mika's mother was nursing her baby son at the time. After he had his mother's milk, Mika replaced him on her back. A few minutes later, Mika noticed many flies around her little brother's mouth. His little mouth was black with flies attracted to the smell of milk.

After the bomb had fallen, there were swarms of flies, lice, worms, and ticks everywhere. They gathered around the carcasses of humans and animals and infested the houses too.

George's hometown is Hiroshima, but he was living in Canada on August 6th and avoided the atomic bomb. Unfortunately, his younger brother and other relatives were all killed. He told me stories he had heard about the lucky ways people had been saved from the atomic bomb. One student was late and missed the train on his way to school. Another had stomachache and spent the day going back and forth to the washroom, and therefore unable to go Hiroshima. One man missed the train looking for his lost eyeglasses; another had a flat tire on his bike so was delayed by repairing it. Those lucky incidents had saved them. The line between life and the death is very thin. One friend told me, "People think I am a lucky person because I am the survivor and living healthily. But sometimes I feel sorry, even feel guilty about my dead friends." Many survivors feel this way. It is a very complicated feeling in their mind.

During the holidays, George and Mika and their two boys went on a trip in his car. I was invited too. I enjoyed seeing the wild animals and the different flowers of this vast country. When we were passing through the meadows along the highway, I imagined there were Apache Indians, riding horses in the hills around us. When I saw the rodeo at Williams Lake I was so excited to see western cowboys wearing cowboy hats and riding horses. They were just like the cowboys in western movies. In September I decided to move to another family and experience life in a different Canadian home.

My Home Stay

At that time there weren't any homestay systems like today. We were referred to as "schoolboy" or "schoolgirl." Some volunteer families offered rooms for a foreign student to live in. Usually there was no charge for room and board but instead the student helped with light housework, washing dishes, cleaning, babysitting, walking the dog and so on.

I placed an ad in the Vancouver Sun saying, "Japanese girl looking for room and board."

I got almost twenty replies from various families. They were very interesting and it took a long time to choose which family I should go to. I decided on Jim and Di Sharp's family. They had three children and Di was pregnant with her fourth child. Jim was a salesman for a pharmaceutical company. Judy was eight years old, Lisa was seven and Danny was three. They lived near the University of British Colombia. I helped Di clean the house, wash dishes, and read books for their children's bedtime stories. My English was poor, but these children listened anyway and frequently corrected my pronunciation. I didn't know the meaning of the word "nostril." This word often came up in one of the stories. I asked them "What is a nostril?" Danny put his index and middle fingers into his nose saying, "nostril." He was so cute. He looked like a little piglet. We all laughed.

The Sharps wished for a baby boy because Danny needed a brother.

They decided to name the baby, "Matthew." I couldn't pronounce "th" sounds because the Japanese Language has no equivalent sound. I practiced saying "Matthew, Matthew, Mathew" over and over again but when the baby was born she was a girl.

They named her Susan, but I started to call her Suki, which in Japanese means "lovable child." They became fond of the name Suki and everyone started to call her Suki, so they officially changed her name from Susan to Suki. Later Suki got married and moved to England where she lived with her husband and two children. Jim and Di continued living in the same house I stayed in for many years. They had five grandchildren and one great grandchild and became some of my most precious Canadian friends.

Cypress Park Tea Room

Chuck's dream was to establish an importing and exporting business between Canada and Japan.

In order to build up capital for his dream business, he started a tearoom called "Cypress Park Tea Room," not far from his parent's house.

The tearoom was located in a West Vancouver residential area near to three other businesses–a drugstore, a gasoline stand, and a beauty salon. Chuck's mother, Margaret, was his right-hand assistant, making pies and serving customers with tea or coffee. It was a brand new business. Everything was new, including stainless steel cooking equipment, a ventilation system, washrooms, and custom-made furniture that had been very costly.

Unfortunately, the location wasn't suitable. There were hardly any customers because it was a quiet residential district. Instead of making money Chuck lost all his investment despite trying his best to make it work.

I was still going to the English school in the morning, and in the afternoon I studied and helped Di with some household chores. Chuck and I met during his holiday or after he closed his store. Sometimes we went to Seattle with his friends to a pub for pizza and a beer. There were six or seven of us packed like sardines in a small car. We would cross the border, eat and drink and come back after midnight. It was a miracle that we had no problems crossing the border and caused no accident or injury by drinking and driving. We also enjoyed cruising in his friend's boat and hiking the nearby mountains. Time flew by like an arrow and my stay in Canada soon reached one year. I was able to extend my visa for another six months.

One night Chuck took me up Cypress Mountain to a lookout spot with a commanding panoramic view of Vancouver. It was a fantastically beautiful night. I'd never seen such a sight in my life. The city of Vancouver's lights were spread under the dark night sky like an endless carpet of glittering, twinkling jewels. They were scattered and sparkling over the entire city. In the harbour was a flotilla of ocean-going vessels. The moon was softly glimmering over the surface of the sea. The top of the hill was chilly and windy. "Oh, I am cold!" I shrugged my shoulders. Chuck held me in his arms and said, "I will keep you warm."

"When can we marry?" I asked him. Silence continued for a while.

"Sachi, let's get engaged. Tomorrow, let's go buy the engagement ring."

I was deeply impressed with the beautiful Vancouver night view. I said, "I don't need any ring. All these glimmering jewels are mine. Whenever I come here, I can look at all my jewels. I would rather marry than have a ring."

"Let's go to a jewelry store tomorrow and you can select your favorite ring," he kept saying.

It wasn't clear if we could marry or not, but we got engaged secretly without telling anyone. Chuck's mother, Margaret was against our marriage. Also, Chuck was not ready to establish a new home anytime soon. Yes, we went to the jewelry store in downtown Vancouver. The salesman showed us several diamond rings from his showcase and put them on the black velvet tray. I had never seen a diamond close up.

'Are those real diamonds?' I thought to myself.

"Which one do you like?" Chuck asked. I couldn't answer immediately. I saw the prices were beyond my imagination. They were very expensive.

"I don't know," I said. Chuck pointed to one ring and said, "How about this one?" It was too big.

"My hand is small so I prefer a smaller size ring that will fit me nicely."

I couldn't decide on which ring to choose.

"Well, I'll give you my suggestion," the salesman said. "Chuck wants you to have a big one and Sachi, you want a small one. How about something between the two?" Then he picked up one from the showcase and put it on my ring finger. How beautiful! Yes, we agreed on it. Since that day, the engagement ring is still shining on my left ring finger.

Barrier of Walls between East and West

In the 1960s immigrants from China, Japan, and many other countries came to settle on Canada's West Coast. The majority settled in the Vancouver area working as fishermen, gardeners and as labourers in the construction of the bridges or railroads.

The most popular job for housewives was that of a cleaning lady. Those immigrants, being new to Canada and coming from non-English-speaking countries, had a difficult time obtaining office jobs. Vancouver had a Chinatown around Pender Street, and a Japan Town around Powell Street. The two Asian communities lived close to each other. While retaining their traditional food and languages, they helped and supported one another in many ways.

Chuck's family home was located in West Vancouver right in front of the ocean. There was an apple tree in the front garden, a small goldfish pond and lots of colourful flowers surrounding the lush green lawn. The house was three stories high, painted green with a dark cedar shake roof and steps leading up to a wide deck on the second story. To me, it looked like a fairytale house compared to a typical smaller Japanese house. West Vancouver was mainly a white Caucasian residential area where most people had a high standard of living. In the old days there was a law in the British Properties area of West Vancouver that Asians could not buy land there.

Chuck's family on his father's side was of German and Danish descent, and on his mother's side, Scottish and English. Occasionally I was invited for dinner or to a party, but I was always the only Asian girl among their gatherings. They treated me as a guest who couldn't understand English. They spoke slowly and clearly, but 1 was often at a loss as to what their conversations were about. Most of the time I imagined what all the talk was about, and in my head made up my own stories. Sometimes my interpretations were wrong and sometimes correct. I often nodded my head saying, "Yes, yes," whether I understood or not.

Chuck's mother was concerned about our relationship and possible marriage because even couples from the same country, speaking the same language and with similar backgrounds, experience difficult problems. Chuck and I were from totally different surroundings, spoke different languages, had different cultures, and religions, not to mention our country's histories and customs. Canada and Japan are absolutely opposite - east and west. Love was the only tie and our only connection.

One day I visited Chuck in his West Vancouver home. When I knocked on the door of his mother's house she appeared surprised to see me. "Chuck went to your house." And she laughed. "What language were you speaking?" she asked. I don't remember how I answered her question. Anyway I asked to stay at her house until Chuck came home because it would take me about two hours to go back to my place changing buses twice. But Chuck had a car and would be back within an hour.

"What do you think that your mother thinks

about me?" I asked Chuck later.

"She thinks you are ambitious," he said. I imagined that meant that I was taking advantage of Chuck. I was getting frustrated being in Canada, and also I missed my family back in Japan. I became homesick so I decided to go back to Japan. I told Chuck that I would go back to Japan and wait for him there.

"I will come too," he said.

"What are you going to do with your Tea Room?"

"I'll close it."

"So soon? It's been only two years since you started."

"It's not at all profitable and, frankly speaking, I'd rather be a customer than an owner. It's enough."

'What a waste!' I thought. In Japan we have an old saying, "Perseverance will win in the end." But for me, it would be so nice to go back to Japan together. On the other hand, I was worried what his family might think about this matter. I wrote a letter to my mother:

Dear Mother,

I am coming back to Japan in September 1964 together with Chuck.

Would you please find a one-bedroom apartment for Chuck in Tokyo, somewhere close to our home. We found a cargo boat in Vancouver Harbour bound for Yokohama. We will land together in Yokohama, and I will stay with you and Chuck will be in his new apartment. We are looking forward to seeing you in September. We have many stories to talk to you about.

Love,
Sachi

One, Two, Three, Jump!

The cargo ship Yamahime Maru, blew its whistle three times announcing its departure from Vancouver across the Pacific Ocean to Japan. Unexpectedly, the cargo ship finished loading early and was leaving one day ahead of schedule. Chuck had gone on a farewell camping trip with friends to the Garibaldi Highlands, planning to be back in the late afternoon the day before his departure. I was in a panic as the ship pulled away from the dock without him.

"We can't help it. He'll just have to get to Japan on his own," his mother said.

"In the Garibaldi Highland forest there are no phones, hotels, or houses so there is no means of contacting him."

I begged the Captain. "Captain, please wait just one day for Chuck. According to the schedule we are supposed to leave tomorrow."

"Well, this freighter is not a cruise ship. When we finish loading we leave immediately for the next destination. Even a day's delay costs big money."

"But please, wait one day. Please!"

"No way. We're not going to wait for only one person even if he's your fiancé."

"Chuck went camping so he doesn't know you're leaving early."

"Sorry!"

I was so disappointed that Chuck hadn't made it aboard before departure. All of his luggage had been delivered to the ship, but we left without him.

Yamahime Maru means "Mountain Princess." In spite of such a beautiful name she was an old rusty tramper of only 3,300 tons. There were ten passenger rooms with a few returning exchange students. We ate every meal at the Captain's table in the dining room with some officers or crew. Missing Chuck, I didn't have much of an appetite. Two days later, at dinner time the captain said,

"Sachi, maybe tonight Chuck may come."

"What? Chuck is coming? How can he come?"

"Everything comes to those who wait."

"What did you say?" I asked.

"Lie in bed till meat falls in your mouth." The Captain said with a smile.

I couldn't believe it. Was this some kind of sick joke? I stepped out on the deck of the boat. All I could see was the dark ocean. Close to midnight the Captain came out on deck and so did other passengers. The Captain pointed far out over the dark ocean and asked,

"Can you see the light over there?"

"Yes, the tiny dot."

"Keep your eyes on it. That's the pilot boat coming to pick up our pilot."

"What is a pilot boat?" I asked.

"The small vessel that brings the pilot who guides the ships in and out of the harbour. It's coming to pick up the pilot. Chuck should be coming with them."

I gazed at the small light. It slowly moved toward the Yamahime Maru. All we could see was a moving light. Is it really a boat? I doubted it until the light was very close. Suddenly a bright spotlight swept over the sea and we could see the pilot boat. Chuck was standing on its bow. The little pilot boat edged alongside the Yamahime Maru. The boat was like a midget alongside the freighter. All of us passengers were squinting down to see what was going on down beside the ship's hull. A rope ladder was thrown down from the freighter deck. The pilot boat heaved up and down over gigantic sea swells. At the top of one swell someone shouted, "Go!" Chuck jumped onto the rope ladder.

"Oh, Ninja!" He scampered up the rope ladder rung by rung.

"Wow!" When he stepped on deck, everyone cheered for joy. Chuck was greeted with handshakes and welcoming slaps on the back.

"Let's celebrate with a welcome party for Chuck." Many passengers and some crew gathered in the salon and I opened the Johnny Walker whisky that I had bought as a gift for my uncle.

"Cheers! Kanpai!" The welcome party continued late into the early hours of the morning. My heart was so happy that Chuck had made it.

How I Came to Miss the Boat — Chuck's Story

"You're too late! It's left." These are the first words I heard from Mom after arriving back at my parents' home from a camping trip with friends.

"Too late for what? What's left?" I asked.

My parents explained the ship I was scheduled to sail to Japan on had finished loading a day earlier than expected and had left port. Strange, I thought. Planes leave on schedule. Trains leave on schedule. How come ships don't leave on schedule? I immediately called the shipping company and was told it was headed for the North Coast port of Kitimat. I called an airline company that flew floatplanes into the nearby airport of Terrace but their planes could not land after dark. It was already mid-afternoon. I then found another airline that had a scheduled flight leaving in a few hours and a seat available. I managed to catch this flight but on arrival found that my ship had already left the final port of Kitimat and was heading for the high seas.

From behind me I heard an excited voice, "Hi Chuck. What are you doing here?" It was one of my mates from Boy Scouts. I explained that I was to catch my ship headed for Japan at Kitimat but that it had just left. My friend then explained that it had to sail down the channel past the port of Prince Rupert and that it might be able to pick me up there.

"I was just dropping my girlfriend off at the airport and now I run into you," my friend explained. "I've got an old sports car parked out front and if you don't mind a windy ride, I can take you to Prince Rupert. It's only 50 kilometres."

We flew like the wind along the dark winding mountainous road reaching Prince Rupert in record time. It was a thrilling ride. The port authority told us the ship was already on the high seas and could not and would not come back for me. However, a small port authority boat was leaving to pick up the coast pilot and if I could convince the boat's captain this was an emergency, he just might take me. I found the pilot boat captain and pleaded with him that I had paid passage on the ship, my fiancé was aboard, and this was my last and only means of getting to Japan. He looked a little reluctant but nodded okay, adding he was not responsible if anything happened.

About an hour or two out of Prince Rupert we came alongside the Yamahime Maru. Huge swells raised the pilot's boat several meters beside the freighter over each crest of a wave then dropped it like a roller coaster into a trough. The captain then gave me some advice. "Study the waves. Study the timing. Keep your eyes on that rope ladder. You're going for that ladder and your timing has got to be perfect. You've only got one chance. Otherwise you'll be in the salt chuck and we can't help you." I'd been in Sea Scouts and grown up sailing and boating in all kinds of weather so I had no fear but lots of respect for the ocean. I knew it could be awfully mean.

"One, two, three – jump." My hands grabbed the rope ladder with perfect timing and with a bag slung over my shoulder, I swung wildly back and forth. I laughed as I pulled myself over the gunnel. A deckhand looked at me with wide eyes.

"Excuse me," I coughed, "but could you kindly show me to the Captain. I have a small delivery." The captain tried to hide his smile and looked at me almost in disbelief. I reached into my shoulder bag, presented him with a bottle of Johnny Walker Black Label Scotch, and said, "Let's celebrate." Sachi stood beside me. She also had a bottle of Scotch. She looked happy.

PART FOUR

Momento Kimono

On September 7th 1965, Chuck and I were married in Tokyo. We visited Hiroshima to announce our marriage to Misao Mother. Then we all went to the Hiroshima Memorial Park and bowed before the peace monument, which has the inscription, "Please sleep peacefully, we will never repeat again." This phrase symbolizes the heart of Hiroshima wishing peace to the world. Memories of the atomic bomb explosion flashed through my mind while I was praying. Every day, every moment, from all over the world, visitors are coming to this site and praying. Each visitor has some silent message for the atomic bomb victims.

'What is Chuck thinking about?' I wondered. 'What is my mother thinking about?'

A few minutes passed then we quietly left. I once told Chuck about my body which had been bathed in radiation from the atomic bomb. His reaction was untroubled, and he seemed not upset at all. This was an incredible relief to me. There is a God!

At Misao Mother's home, she prepared such a huge delicious feast of Japanese food that we couldn't eat it all. As she brought tray after tray of food, she apologized constantly.

"I am sorry I can't make western food. I hope my cooking suits you."

"Mom, everything's delicious. I love everything," Chuck said.

"How happy I am you called me Mom."

"Yes you are my Japanese mother," Chuck said.

She smiled in the midst of tears.

Chuck was wearing a Kimono after a bath and sitting in front of the table enjoying

Japanese dishes.

"That Kimono really suits you. It is one of my husband's best Kimonos. I kept it to give it to someone who is special. Now you're the perfect person for it." Misao Mother offered her husband's treasured Kimono to Chuck as a gift. "Please make yourself at home," she said, as she kept bringing more food.

I was so happy to hear their conversation. How they were peacefully connected even though they had a big culture and language gap.

As night fell, Chuck, myself and some friends went firefly hunting in a rice field near my mother's home. We carried a small cage made of bamboo into which we put some grass for the fireflies. In order to find fireflies, you need good eyesight and have to carefully search the moist grassy bush. The glimmer from fireflies is so minute they're hard to spot but when they're flying across a dark field, they're easy to net. We had a lot of fun trying to chase and catch them. Surely this summer scenario showed the enjoyment of rural nature at its best. We managed to catch several fireflies along a narrow dyke between the rice paddies. When we got home, the dining room had been converted into our bedroom. This is the creativity of compact living in Japan. There were futons, a Japanese bedspread on top of the tatami straw mats. Also there was a linen gauze Kaya mosquito net tent hanging over the futon. We released those fireflies into our Kaya bedroom tent. Their tiny beams of light twinkled on and off. We imagined how aristocrat life in Japan must have been one thousand years ago during the Heian era. The Kaya net futon bed was a fantastic visual experience for Chuck. This happy homecoming nurtured a very sincere relationship between my mother, Misao, and Chuck.

Every year on August 6th, there is a lantern festival on the river in Hiroshima. It is in respectful memory of the atomic bomb victims. Seeing the lanterns floating on the river makes me feel that the victims' souls are at peace. Chuck and I also joined this event the next day. It was a heartwarming moment.

Finding a New Home

"Sachi, I got a telegram from Canada."

"What!"

"The telegram came from my father. He and my sister, Emily, and her Husband are attending our wedding."

"Good news!" I was so excited. But Chuck was shaking his head saying, "What shall I do?"

"Why, this is fantastic news. They are coming all the way from Canada for our wedding."

"Remember, I phoned my father telling him our marriage is in two weeks?"

"Yes, your father was so happy to hear this news."

"Do you know what I said?"

"No, what did you say?"

"Dad asked me about my job, my income, housing, whether I could afford to support a wife and so on." Chuck was shaking his head again. "I told him I had a nice western-style house full of furniture and a lovely garden, so my father sounded satisfied about me getting married. The problem is, I just never ever imagined he'd be coming to attend our wedding."

At that time Chuck was living in an 80 square-foot, one-room community apartment. The room had one small gas burner in a tiny kitchen nook, with no refrigerator, and no oven. There wasn't even a bathtub in the building. All the residents would go to a neighbourhood bathhouse, where for about 30 cents, at that time, they could wash down and take a leisurely, relaxing soak in piping hot water. The common toilet was down the hallway from his room. My mother and I were living in the same apartment building so Chuck was eating meals with us. Some residents had no refrigerators, so my mother offered to share her fridge with these others. Sometimes someone's food would disappear. We never knew who took it or ate it. But it was a friendly community, and we all got along. There were just two weeks to prepare for our wedding. During this time Chuck had to find a new place to live which was supposed to be a western house with furniture. We were both working days at the time. Miraculously, through connections we found the ideal house near the Shinkouenji Station, in the suburbs of Tokyo. The rent was 30,000 yen or about $300 US Dollars. That was almost 10 times more than his one-room apartment. It was a fairly new concrete-block house with a small garden and pond. The owner had his own construction company and built it for himself when he got married. After having two children, he moved into a big house next door. The house had sat vacant for several years so it needed cleaning and repainting. The pond had to be cleaned and refilled, the garden weeded, and flowers planted in order to make it look half respectable. We had problems paying 30,000 yen, which was beyond our budget. We only had a short time to clean the house.

Chuck was determined to take the house. He talked to the owner about reducing the rent in exchange for teaching English to their kids. It was through tough negotiations that the owner's wife finally agreed. Immediately we went to a department store, shopping for furniture. We found a nice dark blue sofa bed that folded down into a bed. "We'll take this one," said Chuck. The clerk sucked some air, bowed and explained that this was a sample floor model and they could deliver one in three weeks. "No time. We need it tomorrow," we insisted. After a little begging and haggling with the clerk's boss, the store agreed to sell us the floor model and deliver it along with a dining table, chairs, some kitchen utensils, and dishes that we'd picked out all at the same time. I tapped my mother on her shoulder, smiled and she paid the bill. After work, Chuck rushed home and painted the whole house. My friends helped me clean inside and out, including the garden and pond. We were all excited and worked hard. Those were hot summer days and we just kept going. Mosquitoes buzzed us and we were constantly swatting them. The second coat of paint on the house was finished the day before Chuck's father arrived. There were goldfish in the pond, flowers in the garden, new furniture and a sofa bed in the house. Chuck acted very relaxed, as he showed his father around the freshly-renovated house. Unfortunately, Chuck's sister, Emily, and her husband, Brian, could not get their visas in time for our wedding so they arrived later.

We Japanese have a saying; "Turn a misfortune into blessing." I wonder if Chuck ever told his father about this.

Television Wedding

Fuji television had a program called "TV Marriage." We applied to be on the show and were accepted. Our wedding was telecast nationwide. "TV Marriage," was an extremely popular TV program at that time. The sponsor was Kao Soap Company, and they covered all the costs of the wedding and honeymoon. The ceremony was held in one of the large studios of the TV station and broadcast live. About thirty guests were invited including relatives, officials from the Canadian Embassy, Nakamura Meiko, a famous entertainer and Tashiro Miyoko, a popular singer whom Chuck requested to attend.

The reason we were selected among many various candidates was that I was a Hiroshima survivor of the atomic bomb and Chuck was a Canadian so this could be called an "International Marriage." A Japanese and Canadian couple getting married was still, at this time, very rare in Japan. The producer could weave an entertaining program around this match. The Master of Ceremonies, Mr. Tokugawa Musei–a well-known celebrity, introduced our life histories with colourful episodes. Prior to the ceremony we had gone on location to Hiroshima for some filming. The producer also planned that we would go to Vancouver to shoot some majestic B.C. scenery but unfortunately the budget was cut. So, on the 7th of September 1965, many of our friends and people who knew us were glued to their TV screens enjoying the wedding show.

Our planned honeymoon to Okinawa was postponed because a major typhoon hit the island at that time. All flights to Okinawa were cancelled. As an alternative, we spent time with Chuck's dad, sightseeing in Japan.

Except for one room that had tatami mats, our new home was a modern western-style house. It was comfortably cozy with a large living room where we frequently invited friends. One of the best things was the deep cedar Japanese furo bathtub. All this came about thanks to Chuck's father suddenly deciding to attend our wedding.

Charles and Sachi's wedding 1965.

The Meeting of the Two Mrs. Rummels

Chuck loved travelling. He had been planning to go on a trip around the world for two years. In 1967, we decided to revisit Canada and visit the Montreal Expo. Our route would be by boat from Yokohama to Siberia. Then by rail across Russia, with a side trip to Outer Mongolia, then through eight Eastern European countries. From there we continued from Yugoslavia, across the Adriatic Sea to Italy and up to Belgium. We didn't have much money, so for most our trip through Europe we hitchhiked and stayed at youth hostels.

Never in my life could I have dreamed of such an adventurous trip. Our route was totally unplanned. Where we would stay each night was a surprise. We were vagabonds. My important role of this trip was hitchhiking, standing at the side of the road with my thumb pointed skyward. Whenever we needed a ride I stretched out my right arm and gripping all fingers, stuck my thumb up in the air and smiled at each driver. At first, I needed a lot of courage to do this queer gesture, but I soon became an expert at getting a car to stop for us. This strange custom seemed to be internationally acceptable but not where I came from. It was an exciting and thrilling moment to find out what kind of car had stopped and what nationality of people had let us join them in their vehicles and where they could take us. From Belgium we found cheap flights to Montreal by way of Iceland and New York.

After arriving in Montreal, Canada, we met Chuck's sister, Emily, and her husband, Brian. They had driven 6000 kilometres across Canada from Vancouver to meet us at Expo '67 in Montreal. It took us all about ten days to drive back to Vancouver, taking in various sightseeing spots along the way. We stopped to tour around the breathtaking Niagara Falls. Then we sped day after day along flat straight roads through prairie wheat farms. Finally, the enormous Rocky Mountains appeared on the horizon. In this vast National Park we stopped to soak in Banff Hot Springs. Wherever we went there were countless spots of natural beauty.

What a vast beautiful country Canada is. 'Every Canadian ought to see this,' I thought.

Approaching Vancouver I got a feeling of anxiety about meeting Chuck's family. I combed my hair and put on lipstick. Then I asked Emily, "Am I all right? I am getting nervous about meeting your family."

"Why? Don't worry. They are all eagerly waiting to see you."

"Are you sure they will accept me as a daughter-in-law and one of your family?"

"Of course they will. We are all happy to welcome you."

The moment when I stepped in the entrance door of the Rummel house, big warm voices welcomed me.

"Hi, Sachi! Hi, Chuck!"

Kissing, hugging and shaking hands, my tiny body was enveloped by the friendly crowd getting together for this welcoming occasion. Chuck's parents' house stood right in front of the Pacific Ocean. I enjoyed inhaling this ocean air so clear, so clean. Chuck's mother, Margaret introduced her relatives and friends to me one by one. This is Fred, here is Sarett and next is Anamae. I repeated their names "Fled, Threat, Enemy." They chuckled politely at my pronunciation. I couldn't figure out why. Chuck's Father, Fred offered me a drink. It was a late summer afternoon. My soul melted into the tranquil surroundings. After a short stay in Vancouver we boarded another tramp steamer and headed back to Japan.

God's Grace

"Congratulations, you have a beautiful baby girl, Sachi," the doctor said.

"Has my baby got all five fingers and five toes?" I asked. "Does she have all her limbs?" I asked again.

"I am stitching your stomach now. I am too busy to check." The doctor was laughing.

'Sounds like everything's normal,' I thought, suddenly felt tired and fell asleep. I had given birth in August 1971, after being married for 7 years. Our little baby was named Lisa Ann Rummel.

She was a miracle baby for us because a doctor had once told me that I would never be able to have a child since my body had been damaged by nuclear radiation. That was a shock. I cried and cried until tears would come no more. However, I never ever gave up my hope of having a baby. I prayed fervently to the Creator, hoping one day He would give me a child.

"Please give me a baby like an angel." I kept praying to the Creator because I strongly believed whoever the Creator was, He would surely give me a child.

One day I visited Ohara Museum in Kurashiki, Japan. I came across the picture called "Annunciation" painted by El Greco. The scene is of the Virgin Mary being told by the Angel Gabriel, about the conception of Christ. My eyes fastened on the scene and could not move for a while. I felt sure I would have a baby.

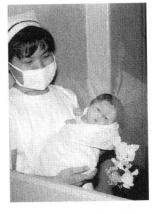

Although I am an atomic woman, I dreamed of a future as a mother. My dream seemed out of reach. But miracles do happen. For only through God's Mercy and His Grace, I gave the birth to a girl, Lisa Ann. Two years later another girl, Tami Sophia, was given to us. These girls are truly miracles of almighty God. Now, as a Christian these Biblical words have special meaning for me.

"Lo, children are a heritage of the LORD: and the fruit of the womb is his reward." (Psalm 127:3)

"The things which are impossible with men are possible with God." (Luke: 18:27)

Being Parents

Lisa Ann was a tiny baby who was 2.6 kg when she was born. The first time Chuck saw Lisa, he was shocked because he had never seen such a tiny baby in his life. He thought she looked like a small creature. He asked the nurse. "Excuse me, is this baby Lisa Rummel?"

"Yes, isn't she cute?"

He didn't answer. His expression seemed puzzled as if to ask, "Are newborns really cute?" Through the windowpane the nurse answered by holding up Lisa in a pink blanket.

Lisa had long eyelashes and big eyes. The thick dark brown hair was curled. She was just like a foreign baby, not at all like a Japanese baby except for the small blue Mongolian spot on her bum which most Japanese babies have.

Often, she became sick and wouldn't drink milk. Sadly, she had an itchy rash on her soft skin. I took her to see the doctor and got some ointment to put on her body. But this rash came on and off and continuously bothered her skin. I wonder whether, because I was the victim of radiation from the atomic air raid, Lisa had received my bad cells. This question arose in my mind and I worried about her health all the time. Doctors could not confirm whether radiation could be a causal factor for Lisa's rash. Even to this day, over forty years later, the itchy rash is still with her.

The Japanese government has declared that second-generation atomic bomb victims' children are not affected by radiation. Do we really know? As a mother, I think this government decision is not satisfactory because not enough research has been done to reach a definitive scientific conclusion. I wish that Japan and the United States would undertake joint research on second- and third-generation children of atomic bomb survivors.

The Blue and Wide Sky

When our daughter Lisa was three years old and our second daughter Tami was one we decided to move back to Canada for the sake of our children. In those days, if the child was born in Japan, they received only the father's nationality but never the mother's. So they were automatically Canadian citizens. Even though they were born in Japan, they would need a Canadian passport and visa. This also meant they could not attend regular Japanese public school even though my husband was a taxpayer. The only alternative was to attend a private or missionary-run International English School where tuition fees were expensive.

The majority of students attending International English Schools had a parent working for a foreign company or their government that would cover educational costs. This was not our situation at the time. Chuck was still a student taking a masters course at

Sophia University. We couldn't afford two daughters' education fees plus Chuck's. We also considered the fact that the Japanese education system, including private schools, were tough and very disciplined.

Chuck wanted to give our children a schooling that was natural with more freedom and fewer rules. On top of this, the housing situation in Tokyo was not great. Our apartment was very tiny. When we considered everything, Canada seemed to be the best place for the children. Luckily, Chuck found a good job with a financial company that would transfer him to Toronto after a couple of years, and we made the move in March 1975. Chuck left for Toronto ahead of us and found us a spacious two-bedroom condominium in an upscale neighbourhood.

Two months later, in April, I landed at Toronto's Pearson airport with our two daughters. I was carrying Tami on my back and holding Lisa's hand. Snow was falling. On the way to our condominium, the snow flurry turned into a wild snowstorm. Visibility dropped to near zero. Chuck was following the taillights of the vehicle in front of us, driving very cautiously. I remember him remarking, "How in the world can people live in such a cold place?" He was from the West Coast where the weather is mild so this was his first experience of heavy snow in April. We were wearing our spring clothes but, fortunately, the car was warm and cozy with the heater going full blast. Snow covered the city. We reached our new home safely. Without ceasing, the snow piled up all night long. In the morning, the sky was clear and blue. The sun was shining.

"Mommy, it's blue sky! Look at the snow. It's beautiful!"

Lisa happily skipped along the sidewalk in front of our condominium. Tami moved step-by-step holding my hand. We had gone for a walk but within 10 minutes Lisa complained, "I'm cold. Mommy."

"Yes, it is cold. Let's go home."

A lady driving along the road stopped her car beside us, rolled down the window and said to us, "Oh, dear, you are wearing such thin clothes. You'd better dress the children in their snow suits They'll catch cold!" Even though the sun was shining, the temperature was minus 10 degrees Celsius. This was something that I could never have imagined. I couldn't figure out what kind of clothes were proper for this strange weather. After all, it was now April. At this time of year in Japan, it's cherry blossom season. People wear spring clothes and picnic under the cherry blossom trees.

Our new life in Canada began when we looked out the window over a garden covered with snow. We used to live in a tiny apartment in Tokyo but now the size of our new condominium was more than twice as big. Lisa and Tami ran all over the spacious living room that was about the size of a little children's playground in Japan. We enrolled Lisa in a private preschool. She couldn't understand a word of English. One day she came home from school and said. "Mommy, I can laugh in Japanese. It's OK."

Tami had a friend the same age who lived in the same condominium. Even though they didn't understand each other's vocabulary, they sure enjoyed playing and fighting together. In the fall, we bought a house in Toronto's suburb of North

York close to Edwards Gardens. Every day I took our two children for a walk to the park. This was our big garden for wandering around under the trees, strolling beside the stream, admiring the flowers, the insects, and breathing in the fresh, crisp air. We met some Japanese and Canadians and gradually our life expanded into the community.

Canadian Citizen

I soon applied for Canadian citizenship. For this I had to study Canadian history, politics, industry and geography. My English was poor but I studied as hard as I could. On the day of the examination, the examiner asked me, pointing to the picture on the wall

"Who is this?"

"Queen Elizabeth." The next question was, "If you become a Canadian, can you vote?"

"Yes."

I don't remember what else he asked me but I only remember those two questions and my answers were correct. I passed! A ceremony followed at the reception room in the city hall. About thirty new Canadians attended that ceremony. After the official speeches, we sang the national anthem together.

O Canada!
Our home and native land!

True patriot love in all thy sons command.
With glowing hearts we see thee rise,
The True North strong and free!
From far and wide,
O Canada, we stand on guard for thee. (At this point I became emotional)
God keep our land glorious and free!
(Now my tears overflowed and I began sobbing)
O Canada, we stand on guard for thee.
O Canada, we stand on guard for thee.

After we finished singing, the girl next to me asked with a dubious look,

"Why are you crying?"

"Don't you feel sad? I have to give up my Japanese citizenship. I lost my country."

"Not me. Not, at all. I don't have a country. My country was taken away by the USSR. Canada is my new country. I am so happy." Her eyes were shining. I thought I should now appreciate being Canadian with a Canadian husband and two Canadian children. But still, Japan is my mother country — full of memories.

My neighbours gathered together and held a

welcome party for me on becoming a Canadian Again I thought how lucky I was to live in a beautiful city, surrounded by good friends. Canada is a peaceful country. I thought, "I should not look back to Japan. I should keep my health in good condition because I have no family or relatives to ask for help in Toronto, Canada. Meanwhile, I should study English. I should take lessons and get a driver's license. Also, I should learn Canadian cooking." These were my resolutions as a new Canadian.

Living with different customs and in a new environment my Canadian life went up and down. But my future would be full of happiness with my Rummel family in Canada.

Another Move

We spent fifteen years in Toronto and adjusted to Canadian life. Lisa and Tami were given their education in English, French and Japanese. Lisa finished grade 12 and Tami was in grade 10. Meanwhile, Chuck's mother, Margaret had passed away. His father Fred, now in his 80s had been ill for a while. We thought this was a good time to move back to Chuck's hometown of Vancouver. If we could live close to his father, it would be ideal to show him that Chuck was a good son. He'd been away for 30 years. Also, I wanted to live in a warmer place and closer to Japan.

Lisa enrolled in Capilano College and Tami attended West Vancouver High School. It was in the summer of 1989 when we made another big move from Toronto to Vancouver. We packed up all our possessions, rented the biggest moving van available, attached a trailer behind with our car on top and in one week drove 4,500 kilometres west to Vancouver.

Rummel family welcome back Alaska cruising 1989

Being an Atomic Bomb Survivor in Canada

The Atomic Bomb Survivor's Certificate is a small pink notebook that identifies my status as being a survivor of the atomic bomb in Hiroshima. I obtained this certificate in 1965. Unfortunately, since I moved to Canada, this certificate became invalid after 2003.

Survivors living outside of Japan were no longer entitled to this certificate. Atomic bomb survivors living in Korea, Brazil, and America took the Japanese Government to court and won their case. Thanks to those who stood up courageously and successfully obtained their certificates, other atomic bomb survivors recovered their certificates. We Canadian survivors also fought against this policy and in 2003, we too recovered our Atomic Bomb Survivor's Certificates. The benefit of this certificate is that if you are travelling in Japan, the General hospitals and special private hospitals will readily admit you for care and hospitalization whenever you are sick, incur an injury, or have an accident. All medical treatment and medication will be free. We are also able to apply to travel periodically to Japan and get a battery of medical exams for health problems — all without cost. In 2014, I hospitalized myself at Hiroshima Red Cross Atomic Bomb Hospital for several days for a health checkup that included a blood test, neck ultrasonography, colonoscopy, neurological examination, brain MRI and so on. In Canada, you would wait at least six months or more in order to get these tests. But within two weeks everything was completed. I've gained confidence now and live a healthy life even despite small problems like high blood pressure, arthritis and pre-diabetes.

There is another good benefit for the A-bomb Survivors living in Canada. Once every two years the mission for Atomic Bomb Survivors group is invited to visit Seattle, to meet with medical specialists from Japan to give us medical check-ups. The specialists include doctors from Hiroshima City and from the Ministry of Health and Welfare. Usually about eight to ten of us survivors charter a bus for the day to take us from Vancouver to Seattle and back. After the doctor's examination and consultations with City of Hiroshima officials, we stop at a Japanese restaurant in Seattle for a late lunch congratulating each other on our long life and wishing to see another again in another two years. Unfortunately, on each trip, the number of the survivors dwindles. Some pass away; others are simply too old to make the trip to Seattle. Nevertheless, this small junket gives us a happy sense of bonding. In addition, the City of Hiroshima sends us an Atomic Bomb Survivor Benefits of about 300 dollars a month. In this way the City of Hiroshima gives great support to us survivors. We are so lucky, and we appreciate all these considerable benefits from Japan, especially from the City of Hiroshima.

PART FIVE

Talking and Writing about my Atomic Bomb Experience

I had always wanted my children and grandchildren to understand my story but it was too painful to talk about. Little by little, I wrote about that day when the big bomb fell on Hiroshima and seeing the big flash that altered my life forever, so one day they could read my notes and understand.

In 2011, when a large earthquake shook the Eastern part of Japan and damaged the nuclear power station at Fukushima, deadly radiation was once again spreading across my birth country. It awoke my own nuclear memories and created within me a strong desire to share my own experience as an eight-year-old girl growing up after the bomb had fallen on my home city of Hiroshima.

Until 2011, I had been one of many women who had kept silent about being an atomic bomb survivor. The painful memories remained as scars on my mind that I didn't like to touch. Like an oyster with a painful grain of sand, I kept it tightly wrapped inside of me, and gradually as years went by, it didn't hurt so much. I got on with my life and covered over the bad memories with many good memories.

In an oyster, over time, that tightly wrapped grain of sand becomes a pearl. So this is how I think of my experience now, a pearl of wisdom to share with the world about the evils of nuclear war and radiation.

From my notes to my children, I started to write articles about my atomic bomb experiences, which were published in Japanese magazines. I realized there was still a great interest in the subject. Many people said, "Why don't you write a book about your experience so more people can understand."

In 2013, with the support of the Christ Congregation that I belonged to, a booklet called 'Let's not forget Hiroshima' was published. However, this booklet was only distributed to the limited people among the Christian fellows of Christ congregation and was never on the shelves of bookstores, or made available to the public, let alone to the world.

Meanwhile, as word spread, I started to receive requests to speak about my experiences from small groups of people who had learned that I was one of the Hiroshima survivors. Most of them were Canadians who did not speak Japanese.

Naturally, I had to tell my stories in English. Although my husband is Canadian, born in Canada, my English was not good enough to tell my stories accurately to English-speaking audiences.

I began to think, "If only I had materials written in English which I could use when speaking in public."

I realized that I needed to brush up on my English so that audiences could understand my atomic bomb stories.

Fortunately, I was living near a public school that taught English as a second language for immigrants, so I enrolled in the two-year program there.

Upon my enrollment, I noticed there were people from all over the world—China, South Korea, Japan, Brazil and European countries like Germany. Some students were professionals such as doctors and IT engineers; others were affluent people who came to Canada on the entrepreneur program, and some were tradesmen, but everyone studied hard because they knew having a good command of English had a direct impact on their income level and enjoyment of living in Canada.

Most of them were young people and it was rare to see seniors like myself. We had classes two nights a week from 6.30 p.m. to 9.30 p.m., and there was homework. I found it especially hard to use a computer in class. However, those two years of study really increased my confidence in speaking English.

Publishing an English Version of My Book

I chose my atomic bomb experience as my class presentation project. My teacher and fellow students encouraged me by saying, "Oh, my gosh, we are so moved by your story! Why don't you publish a book based on this presentation?" But, as I said, my English was still poor.

What should I do? Well, an old Japanese proverb says, "Even those of low ability can outdo themselves when flattered." After giving it much thought, I decided to write a book in English.

First, I started to write little by little with the help of my husband, Charles, my family, and friends. And then, by luck, I was led to specialized people who helped proofread and format my manuscript.

In the summer of 2015, this book "Hiroshima, Memoirs of a Survivor" was published and celebrated with a grand bookaunch party at the Squamish Library on August 6, 2015. I was pleased to receive a lovely letter from the Squamish library thanking me for my talk, which drew the biggest attendance ever at that location. (Appendix 1)

Emi & Kauri my grandchildren holding my first books

Becoming a Storyteller

The story of my atomic bomb experiences spread by word of mouth, and I was given many opportunities to speak, especially at schools. Initially, I met with the Squamish City Education Board in order to make sure that I complied with their regulations for school presentations.

As a result, they really understood my experiences in Hiroshima and referred me to many other schools. My book was also mentioned for Peace Education in social studies and history classes in schools.

I became a 'Grandma Storyteller.' With the support of the community, I began my volunteer journey talking about my experiences growing up after the atomic bomb was dropped on my city, Hiroshima.

Having an English version of my book has been a tremendous help to me when meeting with the board of education and others who wanted to hear my story. Upon reading

"Hiroshima, Memories of a Survivor," they could better appreciate the message I was trying to give.

As a storyteller, there are usually two kinds of groups who ask me to speak: One category is community groups such as libraries, clubs, and churches. The others are schools — elementary, middle, and high schools.

Becoming a grandma storyteller. Credit - Kiyoshi Shimada

My presentation includes my experience living through the nuclear explosion and its aftermath, war in general, the abolition of nuclear weapons, and my hope for world peace.

For community groups, my presentation

would be more like a lecture with many people, but more often it was done in a relaxed roundtable gathering.

In 2015, I was asked to speak at an unexpected venue, the Kendo (Japanese swordsmanship) club in Burnaby, BC. The club was located in "Charles Rummel Park," which had the same name as my husband. The 25-acre park had a baseball field, a stadium, tennis courts, and a community centre. The land had belonged to my husband's grandfather who had donated it to the city a long time ago, and both the park and my husband were named after him.

I thought what a coincidence that I, who was born in Hiroshima, was to give my atomic bomb story in front of people who practice traditional Japanese Kendo at the park that bore my husband's name.

Another location that I remember well was a rural elementary school in Rossland, BC. It was January 2017, our plane landed in the next town due to heavy snow, and we had to drive five hours through the mountainous area to reach the school.

There were twenty students from Grade 3 to

6, all bilingual in English and French. They knew about Hiroshima and Nagasaki's atomic bomb from reading Ms. Sadako Sasaki's book in French. They paid very close attention to my story. I was really moved by their sincere reaction to my story. I could see students with tears in their eyes, as they listened, and looked at me with big, wide-open eyes.

After my presentation, they each made a paper crane and wrote "Thank you. Wish for Peace!" as they handed them to me. The origami crane is the symbol of peace.

Former President Obama folded several cranes by himself and presented them to the Hiroshima Peace Memorial Museum. News of this act crossed the Pacific Ocean, became news in Canada, and encouraged a message of peace.

In middle and secondary schools, there were more students with background knowledge of the atomic bombs dropped on Japan gained through reading books and internet searches. They had informed content in their questions and tended to make comments in relation to world peace. Some had no hesitation in sharing their opinion of my story, such as the email from Ken Hong, who was a Grade 11 student at St. Georges. He said, "In a war, nobody wins. Even though a country may have the advantage of more land or status, ultimately, all citizens involved in the war are subject to torment and pain like you have with your experiences in Hiroshima." (The full letter is in the appendix)

I was so glad and encouraged that my story, even in my clumsy English, could ignite a light of understanding in his heart. I was impressed and relieved to know that there were young men who held such an insightful opinion in regard to the big problems of world history and the struggles for peace.

I found that sharing my story with Canadians, the tragedy of the living in the aftermath of the atomic bomb was beyond their imagination. When they saw the photos and heard my experiences, many people were greatly shocked. It was remarkable for them to see a woman called Sachi who had survived such a horror as Hiroshima standing in front of them.

Maybe it is because Canada has never experienced a major war on its own soil that makes it hard for today's younger generation to understand such a tragedy. They have never experienced the horrors of war, so it's hard to accept that one bomb killed thousands of people and that it actually happened in this world.

This is the main difference compared to us survivors whose atomic bomb experience is literally and figuratively burned onto our minds and bodies.

Another reaction to my survivor testimony was that many Canadians started thinking about how to prevent a similar tragedy occurring in the future.

I think the issue of world peace is better understood in Canada than in Japan since Canada is made up of many ethnic groups.

One Seed

My presentations in Canada have only been supported by the community, my own family, and in Japan by the Hiroshima Peace Creation Fund. It's not a huge contribution to the world, but a modest effort that one person can make.

I tell myself that I am becoming a 'seed sower.' I would like to know that after I have planted my story seeds in as many people's hearts as possible, they will say, "We must never have another Hiroshima again. Nuclear weapons must be abolished."

I want my presentations to be like small seeds that will bloom and flower as time goes by. As my story reaches people's hearts, I hope it will create the buds of a peaceful society that will bloom and create a flowering of peace throughout the world.

When I stand in front of an audience feeling nervous, I hold this belief in my heart, especially when I talk to students at a school who listen enthusiastically to my poor English. I reflect upon my mission 'to become a seed sower' hoping it will make a difference to these children's futures.

I also have hopes that my seeds of peace can also be carried by my book such as is reflected in the email I got from Kazuko Longmuir:

"On reading this book, I had the feeling that I had discovered a flower, blooming in a field burned by war. The author had been an eight-year-old child, living in Hiroshima when the first atomic bomb was dropped and was a witness to this hellish event, which killed her beloved father and other family and friends."

PART SIX

Given a Chance to Live - Two Home Countries

I celebrated my eighty-first birthday this year. When I reflect back on my life, I often wonder how I made it. People who know me well sometimes say, "You have had a life full of drama and drastic events."

Indeed, compared to the life of most Japanese people, my life has taken many unexpected turns, but I have never felt helpless, or that I did not know what to do. In that sense, the term "ups and downs" did not apply to me. I have arrived at this point in my life by believing in letting things take their own course.

When I look back on my life, I think there were five major events:

1) In 1937, I was adopted by a married couple, Kazuo and Yoshiko Shindo, my birth mother's sister, immediately after my birth.

2) In 1945, when I was eight years old, I was exposed to an atomic bomb. I lost my father Kazuo, Aunt Chieko, my relatives and my cousins, and, in an instant, my ordinary happy life was over.

3) In 1965, I married a Canadian, Charles Rummel and, many years later immigrated to Canada.

4) In 2008, I changed my religion from Buddhism to Christianity and was baptized.

5) At 75 years of age, I began giving my atomic bomb presentations in Canada.

Each of these five events was a major change that led me where my life is today.

My life has had many twists and turns and I recently started to feel that I had somehow "been allowed" to live thus far, rather than living "due to my own choices."

I truly feel that I'm here now because I was led by something larger and beyond my own will — probably I was led in this direction by Jesus. Every day I live, I find miracles to be thankful for.

Nostalgia

Giving so many presentations about my early life and writing the book has rekindled strong nostalgic feelings and memories of my hometown and the family that raised me.

Although my life completely changed after the atomic bomb killed my father and caused chaos in Hiroshima, all the memories I have now remain close to my heart, even though they were very painful at that time.

We were poor and did not have enough food or clothes to go around. But, most important, there was warmth in people's hearts despite the adversity.

As time passed, we witnessed the process of Hiroshima's slow recovery: Plants came back among the ruins, houses were built, roads were cleared and even the concrete buildings were reconstructed. The slow breath of resurrection blew into the ruined city.

Even though I have been so long in Canada,

I still read news of my former home in the digital newspaper. I'm happy when I hear that *The Carp*, Hiroshima's baseball team, won the championship in Japan.

When President Obama was in Japan and visited the Hiroshima Peace Memorial Park I was glued to the TV. Nostalgic feelings welled up inside of me. I was moved and impressed by the president's courage and his speech about the dangers of nuclear war.

My husband, Charles and I visited Hiroshima in June 2016, and once again, we felt the voice of the citizens of my former home city wishing for peace, as expressed through the memorial inside the Hiroshima Peace Park. I was especially moved by the writing of a child, who found the hope of peace in a tree that survived the A-bomb. My sincere hope is that Hiroshima remains a city of peace, which continues to appeal for "No More Hiroshimas," the abolition of nuclear weapons, and peace for the world.

A Family for Peace

My birth parents Hisako and Haruki Komura lived in Tokyo and did not experience the Hiroshima bombing. However, I found that my siblings were all somehow involved in the peace movement.

My eldest brother, Fujihiko, who was a professor at Hiroshima University at that time, told me, "Sachi, as a survivor of the atomic bomb, why don't you participate in the peace movement?"

In March 1987, Fujihiko was working with Ms. Sadako Kurihara and about 65 people, planning on writing articles titled "Our Wish for the concept of the Hiroshima Literature Museum," and "Let's Build a Literature Hall of Peace," for publishing in the Chugoku and Asahi newspapers. He wanted to leave behind records on the atomic bomb (literature, materials and documents) to the future generations as a world heritage. But Fujihiko passed away without seeing his dreams realized.

When he was in the Hiroshima National Sanatorium for tuberculosis care, the poet, Mr. Sankichi Toge was his roommate. They talked a lot about literature and Mr. Toge said, "In Hiroshima, there are many kinds of literature written just like a pouring out of one's life and soul."

My second elder brother, Jiyo, who taught physics at Hiroshima University, believed that the nuclear bomb experience should be used for peace.

My younger sister and actress, Toshiko, produced Mr. Sankichi Toge's poem on CD, including "Give Back the Human Race." When I think of it, I am the only one who actually experienced atomic bomb among the Komuras, but my brothers and sisters were involved in the movement for "The Abolition of Nuclear Weapons" and for "World Peace". I was encouraged to learn of my siblings' similar efforts and feel the blood ties.

From the time I was born, I grew up with the protection of the warm love from three families and it still continues to this day. Time heals the troubles and suffering of the past, and I am living every day filled with joy.

Komura family.

Living Within Majestic and Beautiful Nature

Before emigrating, I thought Canada was a part of the United States, and I didn't understand English well, but now it has been over 40 years since I came here. My spirit always feels blessed by the beauty of nature in my new country.

The cultural differences were sometimes a challenge, but gradually I began to understand more about the language, cultures, and customs in my adopted homeland.

And yet, I am still a woman with the heart and virtues of old Japan.

Like most immigrants, I have a foot in both worlds. When I go to Japan, I am often told, "You have become so *Canadianized*, and "It's not so easy to socialize with you."

I may have sometimes failed as a mother, for I was confused by the different styles of parenting and child education between my two countries. In Canada, we do not show our weaknesses and try to justify ourselves. I made a lot of mistakes by not being able to express my opinions and because of my poor English.

When I went back to Japan recently, I reunited with an old friend for the first time in 60 years. He said, "You've become a strong woman at your centre. You remind me of the heart of our daughters of old Japan 'Yamato Nadeshiko,' which has been disappearing in present day Japan. It's just like you came out of a time capsule." It was very rewarding to hear that.

Yamato Nadeshiko, the Pink flower is a poetical expression for Japanese women who look fragile but are strong at their core.

Canada is such a culturally diverse country, very forgiving and easy to live in for new immigrants. People acknowledge and accept cultural differences with open hearts. This non-judgmental attitude helps give hope to immigrants that their dreams can come true in their new country.

You hear all kinds of different languages other than English here, and people have different accents within their own languages. It is so common for people to speak English with an accent without feeling ashamed, and they are even proud of the difference.

I have no problem with my conversational English for everyday life, but still need to study more in order to listen to the lectures and to join in with discussions.

Charles' sisters and relatives tell me, "Sachi, your English is good as it is. Perfect English is not interesting." Is this a compliment or criticism? Maybe a little of both.

It's been 40 years since we moved from Tokyo to Toronto, Canada, and to West Vancouver and then to Squamish, BC, and finally back to North Vancouver. Although located in different parts of the country, each environment had its own charm and beauty. We were blessed with fresh air and water. Each location was a short trip by car to find beauty in natural lakes, valleys, parks and hiking trails that cleansed our hearts.

I was rarely reminded of the atomic bomb tragedy, probably because I had been healed by nature. However, my memories were awakened by the news of the earthquake and tsunami caused by the accident at the Fukushima nuclear power plant in 2011.

This event rekindled my desire for as many people as possible to learn about the horror of the nuclear radiation, how important it is to abolish nuclear weapons, and that this should be my mission for the remainder of my life. We should never repeat the tragedy of Hiroshima and Nagasaki, and I will continue to speak about it as long as my health permits.

The Nobel Peace Prize for 2017 was awarded to a global civil society coalition of non-governmental organizations called The International Campaign to Abolish Nuclear Weapons (ICAN) Ms. Setsuko Thurlow, who was also a survivor of the atomic bomb in Hiroshima, gave a wonderful and powerful speech as a representative of the organization.

Also, the Nobel Prize in Literature 2017 was awarded Mr. Kazuo Ishiguro, who was from Nagasaki. In his speech at the Nobel banquet, he said, "I knew *heiwa,* (peace) the Japanese word I heard from my mother, was something important." The 2017 Nobel Prize Awards went to two Japanese who were from the atomic-bombed cities, and I am so proud of their achievements.

In Canada, we have Remembrance Day, which marks the day World War One ended at 11 a.m. on the 11th day of the 11th month.

We wear red poppies on our clothing and observe two minutes of silence at 11a.m. to commemorate the military victims who died in wars.

For the past two years on the same day, there has been a group called "Vancouver Peace Poppies" which was launched by an English pacifist and commemorates all victims of war. These groups wear white poppies and seek to promote world peace.

I joined their commemoration and laid a wreath as a representative of "The Association For Protecting Article 9" of the Japanese constitution, which promotes peace.

It is encouraging to know that multiple citizens' groups are participating in peace movements to create a better society in the future by dedicating peace garlands to include non-military victims of war.

As a person who has lived through and survived a nuclear bomb attack, I feel the responsibility to share my experience with others. I pray that my own and everyone else's children and grandchildren can co-exist and enjoy living in a future that embraces world peace.

Celebrating my 80th birthday with family in Hawaii.

Blessed are the peacemakers for they shall be called the children of God. Matthew 5:9

Author bio

Sachi Komura Rummel
Photo credit - Manto Nakamura -
https://www.facebook.com/MantoArtworksPhotography/

Born in Tokyo, Japan, in 1937, Sachi spent her childhood in Hiroshima. She was standing under a tree in the schoolyard, three and a half kilometres from ground zero when the atomic bomb was dropped on her city. This experience left her with a profound sense of how precious, yet fragile, life can be.

She married Charles Rummel in 1965 and moved to Canada in 1976. They have two daughters and two grandchildren.

This book is written for young adult readers and all who wish for, and work towards, World Peace.

Appendix

1)   What is an atomic bomb?
What's wrong with it? Dr. Eiichio Ochiai

Atomic bombs were dropped on Hiroshima and Nagasaki, killing tens of thousands of people immediately. Other people died later from radiation. An atomic bomb is using what is called "nuclear energy."

Your body, and whatever you see, touch, smell or eat are all made of atoms, which are tiny, so tiny that you cannot see them. So everything we see in life is made up of millions of atoms combined in many different ways.

There are about one hundred different kinds of atoms. You often hear these days the word "carbon." It is one kind of atom. Our bodies are made of carbon and several other kinds of atoms. You are looking at this page, which is made of paper; paper is made of carbon and other kinds of atoms known as hydrogen and oxygen

Everything on this earth is made of atoms of different kinds.

We cannot see an atom, but many scientists have figured it out that an atom consists of two things — a very small ball called the "nucleus," surrounded by a cloud of electrons (Fig. 1)

An atomic bomb explosion is caused by something that

occurs at the nucleus, so an atomic bomb can also be called a "nuclear weapon." Uranium is the atom on which this action takes place. When another tiny piece of an atom called "neutron" is fired at an atom of uranium, it is split into two smaller atoms, which is called nuclear fission. (See Fig. 2).

*When that happens, an enormous amount of **energy** is released, and this is what makes an atomic bomb explode.*

When used as a nuclear weapon, this large amount of energy coming from splitting the nucleus kills huge numbers of people and destroys buildings instantly. It can also be used to produce electricity in the "nuclear power reactor." This is a peaceful use of splitting the atom.

Most of these smaller atoms created from splitting an atom of uranium are very bad for people's health. They are called "radioactive," and emit harmful rays called "radiation." Different kinds of radiation are known: alpha, beta and gamma rays. If the radiation is strong enough, it can kill people immediately. Many people in Hiroshima and Nagasaki died from radiation as well. What happened upon the explosion of an atomic bomb was that these smaller atoms were produced in a large amount and eventually spread over the entire globe. It is called "radioactive fallout." In Japan it is known as "the ash of death." Many people who survived the explosion, soon started to die from "the ash of death."

The nuclear power reactor, which uses the same uranium and the same principle to get energy in order to produce electricity, also produces the radioactive "bad" atoms. When a nuclear power reactor undergoes an accident it spreads radioactivity into the surrounding area. There have been several serious accidents with nuclear power reactors.

The most recent one was at Fukushima Nuclear Power Plant in Japan, which was caused by the strong earthquake and the huge tsunami that took place on March 11ᵗʰ of 2011 in Tohoku region of Japan. Three nuclear reactors exploded and, as a result, spread out an enormous amount of radioactivity, which has a bad effect on people's health. One serious consequence is the sudden increase of thyroid gland cancer among children. Over the last three years since the accident, 103 children got the thyroid gland cancers in Fukushima prefecture where the nuclear power plant was located. This is over a 100 times more than normal. Also, more people seem to die of heart diseases than normal in the Fukushima area. One of the most prevalent "bad" atoms, called cesium-137, tends to go into the heart tissue and causes heart problems. However, much has yet to be learned about the health effects.

You see that nuclear power is indeed very powerful in producing an enormous amount of energy, which can be used for peaceful purpose as well as military purposes.

But unfortunately it also produces a large amount of the very dangerous atoms at the same time, which hurt all living things including us. So, both nuclear weapons and nuclear power reactors are really dangerous, and I believe should be abolished as soon as possible.

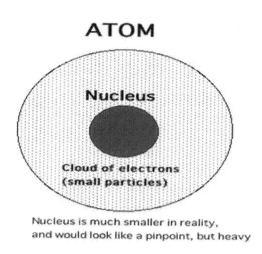

Fig. 1. Atom

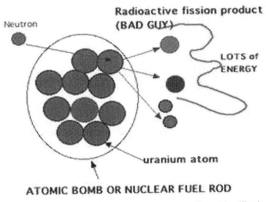

Fig. 2. When uranium atom gets hit by a neutron, it splits into two smaller atoms, which are radioactive, and produces a lot of energy.

2) Squamish Library letter:

On August 6th, 2015 the Squamish Public Library had the pleasure of hosting Sachi Rummel, local author of the book: Memoirs of a Survivor. This event happened to fall on the 70th anniversary of the bombing of Hiroshima. The support from our community for Sachi and her book about the subject was phenomenal.

We had over 70 people attend this evening of discussion

and stories, which turned out to be one of the library's highest attended programs of the year.

It was a pleasure working with Sachi on this event, and I feel her book and her message of peace would be suitable for any library or school program.

Nancy Warwick
Senior Library Assistant

http://squamish.bc.libraries.coop/

3) Summary of Letter from Ken Wong.

Dear Sachi,

I was in attendance at your wonderful presentation at St. George's School yesterday and I briefly spoke with you afterwords indicating my interest in purchasing a book, as well as wishing to purchase a Japanese copy to aid my studies in that language.

Some say that "In a war, nobody wins," and I think that's completely true. Even though a country may have the advantage of more land or status, ultimately, all citizens involved in the war are subject to torment and pain like you have with your experiences in Hiroshima. Likewise, some of my ancestors had been residing in Nanjing when the massacre happened in 1937.

When Barack Obama visited the Genbaku Dome in Hiroshima, and when Shinzo Abe visited Pearl Harbor, some may see it as the re-opening of a new wound. However, I see it as a wonderful gesture — the first step to understanding issues from a less political, but more universal, humanitarian perspective, we are able to better grasp the true suffering contained within these events and learn from our mistakes of the past.

During the past few decades, our world has gradually transitioned to a state of relative peace: from the dissolution of the USSR, to the agreement by many countries for Nuclear Non-Proliferation, we have been making progress, little by little, and fueled by an increasing in education and understanding from all *sides, it seemed that we may just have continued peace for years to come. However nice this may have been, lately there has been a turn away from this attitude on a global scale and a transition back to the hate and division that ultimately fuels war.*

Events such as your workshop and book-reading are able to touch the participants emotionally in a way that a news article would never be able to, so please, keep up what you're doing - continue telling your story for the young people to hear! I certainly enjoyed it a lot.

Many Thanks,

Ken Hong

St. George's School, Grade 11.

4) Letter from Kazuko Longmuir

On reading this book, I had the feeling that I had discovered a flower, blooming in field burned by war. The author was an eight-year-old child, living in Hiroshima when the first atomic bomb was dropped and was a witness to this hellish event, which killed her beloved father and other family and friends. Adopted by family members and thrown into a complicated domestic situation, her life was filled with ups and downs but she never gave in to dark feelings. As we read her story, we are moved from beginning to end by her positive and loving attitude.

Although this is a work of non-fiction, the story carries a strong impact due to the author's truly sweet and gentle personality shining throughout. While this is her first published work, she should be proud to find herself in the company of much more experienced writers. We are left with the hope that this book will be widely read as a compelling argument against war in the continued quest for a lasting world peace.

Kazuko Longmuir

Made in the USA
San Bernardino, CA
16 July 2018